BECOMING FABULOUS

Shine Like the Gorgina Angel BB You (Already) Are

BOOBIE BILLIE

HARPER HORIZON

ISBN-13: 978-0-7852-9057-5 (Ebook)
ISBN-13: 978-0-7852-9056-8 (HC)

Library of Congress Control Number: 2022934022

Printed in India

22 23 24 25 26   REP   10 9 8 7 6 5 4 3 2 1

To Team Boobie. Not bad for two bbs with a dream.

Contents

Introduction

Picture this, bb:

You're strutting down the street in your most fabulous outfit. Your hair is shining and your smile is lighting up the day. Every person you walk by wonders who you are and how they can meet you. Your career is thriving. Your relationships are nourished. Your energy is balanced. You take care of yourself and everyone else around you. Most of all, you feel beyond incredible.

So how did you get here? Well, that's where I come in. Hi, bb. It's me, Boobie Billie. If you know me, we're probably already *very* close. And if you don't . . . well, it's just so nice to meet you! Has anyone told you how *cute* you look today?

And who am I? That's a secret I'll never tell. Just kidding, of course. You may have seen me wrapped up in a towel on your fav skincare brand's feed. Or wearing something ironically fabulous in the digital pages of your fav publication. In mid-December 2019, I posted my very first outfit on Instagram (a photo of me wearing a quilted lilac jumpsuit with matching Nike Cortez sneakers—very streetwear chic).

Since then, I've stomped my way into the fashion world, one little white paw at a time. I've been called Instagram's most fashionable six-and-a-half-pound Italian Greyhuahua. I've built a fabulous community of incredible bbs just like you. I've worked with major brands all over the world. I've even launched a brand of my own. Oof, just thinking about it all makes me crave a vacation. Piña colada, anyone?

Today I sit (metaphorically) in front of you a fully fabulous gorgina angel bb. I own my power. I wear whatever I want. And I take care of myself, no matter what.

It may seem effortless for me now, but things didn't start out that way. It's true, bb. Before the Instagram account, before the iconic looks, I was just a girl, lost and alone in the great big world of New York City. I didn't know who I wanted to be, and I didn't know how to find out. I had big dreams, of course, but no idea how to wake up and make them happen. I knew there was something inside of me—a light so bright it could outshine the New York City skyline. And I was determined to let it out.

So I went on a journey to find my best self. I looked high and low. I looked in the boutiques of the Lower East Side and the cafés of Soho. I looked in the halls of prestigious fashion institutions and in sultry dark corners of art galleries. I looked in the hard-core workout classes, through glasses of green juice, and in the comforting arms of some gorgeous company.

Everywhere I looked, I found something. A statement bag here. A fabulous life lesson there. All these gorgina little puzzle pieces that, when brought together, made up the stunning masterpiece of who I truly am. I found that working hard and playing harder is just simply not the recipe for a beautiful life. In fact, it's a surefire way to deplete your energy (and develop eye bags). I found that nothing's more important than the people you love—and that when you forget this, the people you love have to remind you. I found that not everything has to become a side hustle. In fact, sometimes doing nothing is the best thing you can do. And as it turns out, I've learned I'm not the only one on this journey. The more I grew my community, the more I realized that we're all just trying to give our most fabulous selves the chance to see the world. So that's what led me here, right to the intro of the book you now hold in your hands. (Love that polish color, by the way.)

Because the truth is, bb, your most fabulous self is already within you. And I'm here to help you let it out.

Maybe you're an at-home fashion icon, looking for the courage to wear that wild piece out. Maybe you're the next big CEO, looking for a way to have it all. Or maybe you're just a bb looking for the little push you need to live your dream. Whatever it is, I've got you. I've made mistakes and learned lessons the hard way so you don't have to. Through trial and error, fashion faux pas, and self-care disasters, I've learned the power of taking care of myself—because if I don't, who will?

I've learned to listen to me and *only* me. And I've learned how to feel comfortable being a little extra. Because when everything is extra, nothing is, bbs.

But this isn't about me. It's about you! By the end of this book, you'll have literally everything you need to become your own gorgina angel bb, to take care of yourself and all the queens around you. Spoiler alert: It's all within you already. So grab your coziest dollop of blankets, put on your fav rejuvenating mask, and blast your feel-good playlist. It's going to be a *stunning* ride.

💜 Love you, bb—
Boobie

Official Bb Status

Years ago, I was talking to a very special friend of mine. We were discussing friendship and how we wished there were more official terms of endearment for friends like there are for significant others. Sure, you can use *babe* or *hun*, but for me those just never felt quite right. We were playing around with different words, half kidding. We threw around silly options like *lala* and *bestianna*. Then out of nowhere, she said "bb." It was perfect. And just like that, the bb was born.

From that moment on, *bb* was the way we referred to each other and to any other bbs we loved. Then it blossomed into more. It became a sign of like-mindedness, like, "I see you, bb. I love what you're doing, and you belong here with me!" It became an unspoken, spoken, secret, not-so-secret club. But one that everyone was invited to join, of course.

So consider this your very formal invitation. You officially belong to a group of fabulous people I hold very dearly and would do anything for. And with this official bb status comes very official bb responsibilities. So put one hand over your beautiful heart and repeat after me:

I, bb, swear to always strive for fabulousness
in all my endeavors.

I swear to always be there to spice you up
when you're feeling low.

I swear to always say something if your outfit
doesn't work. (I mean, you can pull
off anything, but I'm talking about
emergencies here.)

I swear to *never* talk behind your back, unless
it's to give you compliments, of course.

I swear to always tell you the truth, even if
it's hard. Like if you've walked around
all day with spinach in your teeth.

I swear to never let society's so-called rules
hold me back.

I swear to wear any color and any pattern
that speaks to me no matter what,
including white after Labor Day.

And most importantly, I swear to do
everything in my power to let my best
self shine and to help other bbs do
the same.

And with that, you are an official bb. Welcome to the
most fabulous club in the world. Of course we have jackets.
And you'd better believe they are gorgina.

The Official Bb Glossary

I've never been one to stick to the usual parameters of language. You know me, bb, always making everything my own. So throughout this book, you will see me using a few official bb terms quite liberally. Some you might already know. Some might be brand-new to you. And some might seem a little out-there. But you know what, bb? That's where we like to be. Because nothing fun ever came from staying within the bounds of what's usual.

So to avoid any confusion going forward, I've put together a little bb glossary. Read it, memorize it, and get ready for a pop quiz at the end of the class. Kidding, bb. I would never do that to you. Besides, you already passed with flying colors! But feel free to use these outrageous bb words to add a little spice to your everyday life. Trust me: They make everything a little more fun. Just try not smiling as you read it.

Gorgina: Something particularly stunning—like gorgeous but on another level and without the seriousness. For example: *Omg, bb, your new haircut is just absolutely gorgina!*

Gorgina angel bb: An absolutely beautiful person. Someone who always lets out their true self, who radiates fabulous energy, and who never lets anything get them down. Someone who's always there for you and is just genuinely amazing. For example: *Wow, she planned your entire birthday party? What a gorgina angel bb.*

Bb: A casual way to refer to someone who is just soooo special to you. Someone close to your heart—a person you admire, love, and appreciate for who they are. For example: *Ugh, bb, you never cease to amaze me.*

Queen bb: The absolute *height* of bbs. The crème de la crème, the upper echelon. Truly bb royalty. For example: *Ariana Grande is the original queen bb.*

Literally: Probably something not literal at all. A way to set up some massive exaggeration and help make it *so* clear that you're just *not* kidding whatsoever. For example: *Those Manolos Carrie wore literally killed me, bb. Like, literally stomped all over my heart!*

Extravaganza: Originating in drag culture. An explosion of extravagant gorgeousness. An experience or outfit that is just so perfect and incredible that it can be described in no other way. For example: *I'm wearing just an absolute tangerine extravaganza to the wedding. Orange on orange on orange, bb.*

Fabulosa: Fabulous but with flair. For example: *Are you coming to the party tonight? I hear it's going to be absolutely fabulosa.*

Eleganza: Originating in drag culture. The height of elegance, stylishness, and sassiness all wrapped into one. For example: *Tonight we're going full prom queen eleganza, bb. You'd better bring it!*

Glamazon: A truly glamorous, self assured bb. Not necessarily tall, but tall in stature. For example: *Ugh, you are an absolute glamazon in those platform heels!*

Smize: A coy, modelesque smile with the eyes. The Tyra Banks–approved way to become America's Next Top Model. For example: *Okay, model bb, I see you with that smize.*

Dollop: An exceptionally fabulous way to be wrapped up in a cozy textile, making one look like a perfect little drop of whipped cream. Effect can be achieved with a blanket, scarf, or plush towel. For example: *I'll be curled up in a dollop all weekend. Don't call or text.*

Farm girl chic: A rustic, farmer's daughter–inspired outfit but made totally fabulous. Usually includes a mix of gingham, small florals, or plaid. For example: *Did you see Dorothy the other day? She was giving farm girl chic and I'm living.*

Boobushka: A little grandmother-inspired headwrap moment that can make any outfit look chic. Like a babushka but more me. Pairs perfectly with old-school Cadillac convertibles and sunglasses. For example: *Throw on your Pickled Zebra Boobushka and a fabulous pair of mini glasses. We're going on a road trip.*

C-sweety: An absolute boss of a bb, who stomps their way into the C-suite and takes it by storm. The perfect way to tell someone close to you that you think they're just absolutely brilliant and destined for success. For example: *Omg, you were* made *for that promotion, you little C-sweety.*

Lewk: Not just an outfit, but a perfectly crafted combination of colors, patterns, trends, and accessories all coming together to create a true iconic moment. For example: *I saw the pics of you from last night. What a lewk.*

Lewwwwwwwk: The absolute highest level of a lewk. For example: *Did she really just show up in the new UGG X Telfar bag? What a lewwwwwwwk.*

Ugh: A way to express a level of appreciation and admiration that is truly beyond words. For something so incredible that language is just not enough. For example: *Um, excuse me, but that top?* Ugh, *bb, I'm living.*

Ugh: A way to express a level of unappreciation and dissatisfaction that is truly beyond words. For something so incredibly not cute that language is just not enough. For example: *Um, excuse me, but he said what?* Ugh, *bb.*

Weekend identity: The personality you assume from 5:00 p.m. on Friday till 9:00 a.m. on Monday. It can change every weekend, depending on your mood. For example: *I was giving major sleepy bb weekend identity on Sat.*

Fantasy: A very specific vision or dream moment to lean into. Something extravagant or fabulous to try on, like a new persona for a day. For example: *She's living her upscale Lower East Side girl fantasy with that stunning Susan Alexandra purse.*

Manifesting: Making a fabulous, iconic dream come true. When success seems like it just came out of nowhere but truly took many little steps to bring to life. For example: *I see you manifesting your business bb dreams, and I'm here for it.*

Friday night uniform: That very specific look you slip into as soon as the clock strikes 5:00 p.m. on a Friday. Could be a cute matchy loungewear set or a fabulous, chic dinner look, depending on your plans for the evening. For example: *I'll be there in five—just changing into my Friday night uniform.*

Hot bb winter: Like hot girl summer but for those months that are a little less hot. A way to embrace the long, cold days and shine through the darkness. For example: *Throw on that fabulous oversized turtleneck. It's hot bb winter!*

Power turtleneck: An iconic turtleneck moment that turns anyone into a powerful tech CEO. From Steve Carell to Steve Jobs in a snap. For example: *Wow, you killed that presentation. Must have been the power turtleneck.*

Mood: The perfect way to describe the current energy of the moment. Can be used sarcastically or seriously. For example: *Current mood: wondering if Rihanna and A$AP Rocky will adopt me anytime soon.*

Moooooood: A way to describe anything cow print that's just fully the mood. For example: *That cow print bag is a moooooood.*

POV: A way to show someone a new perspective. Usually not a serious one. For example: *POV: I'm the lip gloss you always forget in your mini bag.*

Moment: The current situation. Something that is so absolutely right now. Can also be used to describe something that's just so elevating it takes over the entire present. For example: *That green GANNI hat with that matching Prada bag is such a moment.*

Beyond: Miles away from the moment. A way to stress just how incredible something is. For example: *That charcuterie board was absolutely beyond.*

Giving: What an outfit, person, or moment is reminding you of. For example: *That yellow coat is giving Big Bird chic.*

Living: Loving something so much it practically becomes the reason you are alive. For example: *I'm literally living for this new season of* Euphoria, *bb.*

Top shelf: The shelves in your bathroom where you keep your very best beauty and self-care products. Something to show off and be proud of. For example: *My top shelf is looking a little empty these days. Time for a Sephora run.*

Miami Vice Queen: A bright, neon bb who's just giving eighties iconicness while still being ahead of their time. For example: *Okay, Miami Vice Queen in that neon-orange jumpsuit!?*

Angle: That go-to stance or face tilt you hit when you want to make sure you look gorgeous in a picture. For example: *You were really hitting your angles in that last Insta photo dump.*

Galaxy: When you're wrapped up in so much gorgeous fabric you shine like the center of a galaxy. For example: *This scarf is such a satin galaxy.*

Sun bb: A bb who can't get enough of the sun. For example: *Please move that beach umbrella away. I'm a total sun bb.*

Groundbreaking: Coined by Miranda Priestly in *The Devil Wears Prada*. Can be used sarcastically or as a way to show just how new something is. For example: *Florals for spring? Groundbreaking.*

Lush: Something divine and extravagant. Plush and luxurious. Could be something in nature, but not necessarily. For example: *Heard you had a little spa day yesterday. So lush, bb.*

Color-blocking: A way to maintain outfit harmony by wearing blocks of color rather than a mixed-up rainbow. For example: *Green boots, green pants, a blue cardi, and a blue turtleneck. What a color-blocking queen.*

Pattern-clashing: A way to maintain outfit harmony by intentionally picking patterns that clash. For example: *I'm gonna pattern-clash some mega plaid with some micro florals today.*

Monochromatic: An easy bold look created by wearing multiple shades of the same color. Can be done with neutrals, but looks even better with bright colors like purple or green. For example: *A monochromatic all-purple look, and suddenly lilac is a neutral.*

Scandi-funky: An aesthetic inspired by the simplicity of Scandinavian cuts and textures, filled in with bold, funky patterns and colors. For example: *My new KJ Plumb scarf is sooo Scandi-funky.*

Groutfit: An all-gray outfit. Gray on gray on gray from head to toe. For example: *I've worn this athleisure groutfit every day this week. And you know what? I've never been happier.*

OOTD: The outfit you've chosen to wear on any given day. Literally translates to *outfit of the day.* For example*: My OOTD is full-on* Clueless *chic in this plaid mini skirt.*

OOO: Out of office, but like waaaaaay out of office. Not for a sick day but for a fabulous, intentional step away from work. For example: *I'm OOO this week in Tulum. If you need me, no you don't.*

CHAPTER 1

Wear What You Want

Picture this, bb:

It's sometime in the past. The sun is shining. Life is simple. The only mask on anyone's mind is a resurfacing clay mask. Sia's "Chandelier" plays in my tiny Williamsburg apartment. The place is very Scandi-funky, lightly decorated with a mix of birchwood and bright colors. I throw open my disorganized closet to get dressed for the day, and there it is: a sea of black. Black cropped jeans. Black chunky turtlenecks. Black sandals. Black boots. All. Black. Everything.

I know what you're thinking. *Boobie Billie in* all black*? But you're such a color-blocking, pattern-clashing queen! How could this ever happen? Who hurt you?* Trust me, bb, I know. But it's true. For a long time I was terrified of wearing anything other than black. Every day I would put on my monochromatic uniform, grab a tall iced coffee with regular milk (this was the time before the great oat milk revolution, bb), and go to my internship at *Vogue*. I walked the halls anonymously. I slipped in and out of meetings unnoticed. I was so afraid of being seen, and my all-black outfits helped me blend in. If I didn't step out looking like a gallery owner on the way to Morticia Addams's funeral, I just didn't feel right.

My little all-black wardrobe did its job for a while. And not just visually. The dark, moody outfit vibes basically gave me permission to be a reclusive, quiet bb who wallowed in her inner darkness. If I was nervous in a meeting, I could pretend

I was in the shadow of the fabulously dressed people in the office. If I was feeling shy at a launch event, I could channel my inner diva, make a little scowl, and tell myself, *If anyone sees me, they will think I am a mysterious fashion glamazon model.* Spoiler alert: They didn't.

One evening, I was attending a work party at this gorgeous brownstone in Manhattan. It was a farewell send-off for one of the long-standing editors, and everyone was going to be there. (Sidenote: I really cannot stress enough how stunning this place was. It was like a sophisticated it-girl's Pinterest board exploded and landed in the absolute perfect places. Like, in one corner was a matte-white Romanesque plinth covered with small Japanese-inspired pottery. In the next, a handwoven tapestry draped above a bright, burnt-orange couch. Honestly, bb, it was a true masterpiece of interior design and one of my favorite spaces in the world.) (Sidenote to the sidenote: The key to bringing different vibes together is a consistent subdued color palette with intentional moments of pop. Simply divine, bb.)

Anyhoo. Back to the soiree. The moment I walked into the room, I felt out of place. The room was filled with the Who's Who of the *Vogue* empire. And to no one's surprise, they all looked fabulosa. Ornately patterned pencil skirts. Vibrant, Miami Vice Queen oversized yet tailored blazers. Jewel-toned cocktail dresses. And so many actual jewels. It was as if all the exquisitely dressed mannequins at Barneys (RIP) had come to life to celebrate their beauty. And then there was me, standing in the corner, clad in my fail-safe onyx safety blanket. I'm talking a black chunky oversized knit turtleneck, layered over a pair of black flared pants, with four black mules to match. A true moody masterpiece.

I slinked around the room nervously, tracked down a waiter, and grabbed a little glass of pinot noir—the perfect drink to complete my energy. Instead of pulling myself up by the mules and mustering up the confidence to be the bright bb I know I am, I did the exact opposite, sinking further and further into my protective shell. I slid in and out of conversations, laughing quietly at jokes and moving on just as quickly as I had arrived.

Until I found a group of people I recognized. They were all listening intently, gathered around someone I couldn't yet see, like some unseen person was telling them the meaning of life. As I slid closer, I realized the person holding everyone's attention was my boss. I smiled at her as she wowed the group with her fabulous industry stories. And truly, bb, I was in awe. She was absolutely captivating, right down to her outfit. She wore a hot-pink chiffon milkmaid dress, with matching hot-pink heels and a hot-pink lip. It screamed "Pay attention to me or else!" in the very best way. In that moment, the two of us could not have been any more different. Her, this bold, confident, colorful person, outside and in. And me, quiet, nervous, unsure, and fading into the background.

The night went on, and I found myself taking in a moment of fresh air alone on the balcony, breathing out a bit of my nervous energy for the first time that evening. Just as I reached a moment of calm, laughing partygoers spilled out on the balcony and continued their loud, joyful conversation under the night sky. I stood there for a few moments eavesdropping and keeping to myself, but I was getting a little chilly. As I started to move back inside, shuffling past them to reach the sliding balcony doors, I heard a familiar voice call out, "Omg, Boobie, is that you? When did you get here?"

It was my boss. I had literally stood in her circle for—what, an hour? How was she just seeing me now? Was I, like, invisible or something? She came over to my side of the balcony and we chatted for a while. Her, still completely under the impression that I had just arrived at the party. And me, too nervous and shy to tell her that I'd been standing with her the whole time. But I really couldn't blame her. In my all-black outfit, I was easy to miss.

A few weeks later, everything changed. It was a day like any other. I was strolling down the streets of Soho, wearing yet another all-black ensemble. This time it was a black pleated miniskirt and an oversized crew, layered over a crisp black oxford. Oh, and a black mini bag, but like, of course. Very prep school chic, if you ask me. I was taking a sip of my iced coffee when I almost spit it out, right into a very stylish woman's face (sorry, lady!). There in the window of the boutique du jour was the most beautiful coat I'd ever seen: a lilac trench coat.

No. *The* Lilac Trench Coat. She was light, powdery matte lilac with matching buttons and wide sleeves. Her collar was more dramatic than a Netflix dating show, with a slight flare at the back. Bb, she was absolutely gorgina. The way she stood out on that busy block. How she turned that lifeless mannequin into an it-girl. Standing there in my all-black OOTD, I couldn't believe my tiny eyes. I didn't know who she was or how much she cost, but I knew I had to have her.

Did I black out? Because before I knew it, I was in the boutique standing in front of a full-length mirror with the trench wrapped tightly around me and the saleswoman telling me just how good it looked. The coat was even better than I could have imagined. She was practically glowing, brighter than anything I'd ever owned. She was drama. Eleganza. She made me feel like a pastel-purple Carmen Sandiego. And just like Carmen, I was ready to take on the world.

Back home, I parted the sea of black in my closet and hung the Lilac Trench. And all of a sudden, my wardrobe felt brand-new.

The next morning was a beautiful one. There was a slight summer breeze, and like some kind of miracle, almost no humidity in the New York City air. I stomped out of my apartment wearing the Lilac Trench. And, bb, it felt like a dream—only I didn't have to wake up from it. Do you remember the opening scene of *The Devil Wears Prada*, where all those fabulous women get dressed for their fabulous jobs? Well, bb, that's what it felt like wearing the coat. Suddenly I see!

As I walked to work, I noticed something: people were looking at me *differently*. Did my grumpy neighbor fail to scowl today? Did that cute barista actually make eyes at me? Did that rat on the subway scuttle away to make room for me? I felt like a new woman.

And at work, things got even better. People were noticing me—and no one *ever* makes eye contact with interns at *Vogue*. As I took coffee orders, I was funny and outgoing. As I pulled pieces from the closet, I was bold and sure of myself. One of the stylists asked where I got my coat. But that wasn't even the best part, bb. Around lunchtime, I was in the elevator, holding a stack of issues to bring up to the main floor, when it happened. The moment I'd been waiting for my entire time at *Vogue*, and maybe even my entire life. The elevator doors opened, and in walked Anna. Yes, that Anna. She took one look at me, lowered her glasses, and nodded. A full up-and-down of her iconic, bob-haired head. Bbs, my life was complete.

That night, I floated back to my apartment after one of the best days of my life. I sat down with my "Big Dreams" journal and started to reflect. Just what was it about this coat that had such an effect on me and everyone else? Was it the cut? Did it complement my ears? Or had I just walked around with kibble in my teeth all day? No, bb. It was something more. It wasn't just the coat and how it made me look. It was who I became on the inside when I wore it.

See, I had been wearing black for all the wrong reasons.

It was never about looking chic or edgy (even though you can defs look chic and edgy in all black). It wasn't a moment of glamour or timelessness. I had been wearing all black because I was afraid to stand out. To let anyone truly see me. I wanted to blend in because I was worried people wouldn't like what they saw if they *actually* saw me. I wanted to fade into the background, because it felt more comfortable than stepping into the spotlight.

But that's not me. Not even one bit. Ask anyone who knows me well, and they'll tell you that deep down, I'm a colorful bb at heart. I know I'm a vibrant, funny, bright person. My energy is blue and pink and green and purple. Sure, it's okay to mix a neutral in there at times, but I know my heart is more technicolor. For years I held myself back, too afraid to show the world the real and colorful Boobie, afraid they wouldn't like the shade. But it was time to let the world see my true vibrant self, inside and out.

After the Lilac Trench Coat, I knew I needed more. More coats? No, bb. More color. The Chartreuse Turtleneck, then the Red Miniskirt, then the Yellow Sundress, and so on—until my entire wardrobe was bursting with color. The more bright, colorful pieces I got, the more confident I felt. The more I stood out, the more I wanted to stand out. In hot pink, I took up space. In turquoise, I made myself known. In cobalt, I could walk into a room and really be there. And I loved it. No more hiding behind a cloak of darkness. I'm here, bb. And you'd better pay attention.

So to any bb out there hiding behind their all-black (or any other neutral) wardrobe, I say this: You look chic, bb. Honestly, you always do. But ask yourself a few questions: *Am I wearing neutral colors, or are neutral colors wearing me? Do I worry about standing out because I don't want to draw attention to myself? If my personality was a piece of clothing, would it match what I'm currently wearing?* Think about the *real* reasons you're wearing what you're wearing, and if the answer is anything other than *I love it all*, it's time for a little shake-up. Life's too short to not be the person in the room who makes everyone think, *Wow, who is that?* You want to be the one they can't get out of their heads—not the one they forget was even at the party.

So where do you start? Well, simply. Find your version of the Lilac Trench—a bright, colorful, loud piece that absolutely *screams* at you. Maybe it's a cheetah-print blouse or a Bottega-green pencil skirt. Maybe it's the two together. Ooooh, actually, that would be pretty stunning. Whatever it is, wear it out *immediately*. Do *not* let it sit for years in the back of your closet with the tags still on. Wear it to a coffee shop, the grocery store, or the gym (maybe not if it's the pencil skirt, tbh). Honestly, it doesn't matter; just make sure the world sees it as quickly as possible. Then notice how it makes you feel. Notice the changes in your energy. Notice how the color on the outside lets out the color on the inside. And slowly but

11

surely, watch yourself transform into the luminous, bright bb you were always meant to be. Because if there's one thing I know to be absolutely true, it's that dressing for yourself is *way* more fun than dressing for anyone else. If you're out there wearing something that makes you feel truly seen, the world will notice. And who knows? You might just inspire another bb—someone hiding behind their all-black wardrobe—to do the same. So, bb, just wear what you want.

Stop wearing clothes and start wearing *looks*

Okay, but like, do you love it?
Then wear it

Technicolor is the new black

Are they staring, bb?

Who says colors are seasonal?

HOT TIP:
Wearing one bright color from
head to toe makes it a neutral

If you're looking for a sign to wear that gorgina piece with the tags still on

There's no such thing as too many shoes

Gucci in the grocery store? Why not?

Find what makes you feel powerful and *wear it*

Don't follow trends; follow your truth

Dress for the life you want

Don't let anyone tell you what to wear

Not even me

Fashion isn't about rules

It's about breaking them

STEP 1:

Find your power color

STEP 2:

Take over the world

CHAPTER 2

Take Care of Yourself

Picture this, bb:

It's 6:30 a.m. on a Tuesday, and I'm already up, getting ready for another day of living the dream. I'm a regular working woman, except my nine-to-five is more like an eight-to-ten. My internship turned into a full-time job as an assistant, which turned into a full-time job as a junior stylist / coffee fetcher / jill-of-all-trades. Of course, this is fashion: if you're not wearing lots of hats, you won't stand out. I regularly stay up all night working on presentations, fueled by nothing but coffee and couture. I lead meetings on no sleep, owning the room as if I was born for this (which I was) and hoping no one notices I'm wearing the same clothes as yesterday. My photoshoot ideas are getting chosen. My styling is getting noticed. I even land a cover shoot—something that is absolutely *unheard of* for someone at my level. I'm also covering fashion weeks, meeting my idols, and going to all the events. By day, I'm officially *in*. And by night, I'm going *out*. After-parties, bars, pre-showings, and restaurant openings. It's all part of the job—rubbing shoulders and wagging tails with the Who's Who of the fashion world.

I was living the glamorous fashion lifestyle I had always dreamed of, bb. Sure, I had eye bags, but at least mine were Chanel. To most, it would seem like I was doing well—thriving, even. But on the inside, something was changing. Like at an emotional level, but also a gut health level. It was subtle at first. A missed Pilates class here, a few too many late nights there. I knew I was tired, but I was young! Wasn't staying out late what a one-and-a-half-year-old was supposed to be doing? *This is my time to go wild,* I told myself. So I kept going.

I took on more projects and put more pressure on myself. I kept saying yes not because I was passionate but because of how I knew it would make me look. The busier I got, the less I took care of myself. I stopped eating well, swapping nutritious meals for quick comfort-food fixes. Don't get me wrong; I love Williamsburg Pizza as much as the next bb. But when it became a go-to rather than a treat, it stopped being cute. Then, I stopped exercising because *God forbid* I take an hour out of my precious day to stay active.

I even stopped washing my face at night. Ugh, I know, bb. I went from a meticulous ten-step beauty routine to being one step away from using conditioning shampoo. I can hardly believe it either. Because of all the not-so-gorgina stress, my beauty rest grew a lot less beautiful. Sure, the nineties glamour-grunge bag-under-the-eyes look is sexy on some, but I wasn't Courtney Love-ing it.

That time in my life was a stressful blur. But one moment stands out vividly, like a hot-pink Telfar on an all-beige outfit. On the morning before a huge shoot we had spent the last three months planning, I woke up a little late and was already behind schedule. *So* behind that I barely had time to do even a no-makeup makeup look. I wolfed down a croissant, fluffed my ears, and ran out the door, but not before spilling a little coffee on my blouse. Just what I needed . . . not.

The shoot was at the Ludlow, a super iconic hotel I could only dream of resting at. I pulled up in a cab (no time for subway antics today, bb), flew out the back, and ran toward the door. *Beeeeep!* I turned around to see the cabbie frantically waving me over to collect the phone I'd left in the back seat. Ugh, bb. I thanked him profusely and continued sprinting toward the location. I glanced down at my phone for literally one second to text my boss that I would be right there, when all of a sudden I was on the ground, the contents of my purse scattered out around me.

Oof, that hurt, bb. But there was no time for pain. I had a shoot to get to! I was picking up my fallen purse staples—lip gloss, wallet, sweet potato treats—and putting them back in my bag when I realized what had caused my fall in the first place. I had run headfirst into a woman who was also now on the ground, picking up *her* things and putting them into *her* bag. And that's when I noticed her Birkin bag. And a certain extremely recognizable lion tattoo on her finger. It couldn't be.

I looked up. It was.

It was the insanely famous supermodel we had booked for the shoot. *Oh God,* I thought. *I've ruined everything for sure. She's going to hate me all day and the shoot will be terrible. Then my career will be terrible. Then my* life *will be terrible!*

My heart was pounding. I apologized profusely, nervously rambling something about packing up her bag myself when she stopped me. She cracked a smile. "I guess this is the part in the movie where we lock eyes and fall madly in love."

We both burst out laughing. To my surprise (and relief), she was super nice. We finished gathering up our stuff and walked together to the shoot, chitchatting the whole way. I complimented her bag, and she told me she loved my top (despite the coffee stain). We talked beauty routines and our mutual love of rom-coms. By the time we walked in, we looked like BFFs. My new supermodel friend and I gave each other a little French double cheek kiss and went to our respective departments—her to hair and makeup, where she would continue being a glamorous goddess, and me to where my boss angrily awaited me, tapping her foot impatiently as I approached.

Catching on to her less-than-good vibes, I started to explain what happened. She waved me away before I could get anything out. "Boobie, I don't need your life story. Just start steaming the second look, okay?"

I nodded and turned on my paws to leave, but she stopped me. "And Boobie, one more thing . . ." She stared at me for a second, then sort of tilted her head to the side. "You look really tired." And with that, she walked away.

Greeeeat. Exactly what I wanted to hear after spending the last few minutes with a supermodel. I bet *she* thought I looked exhausted too. Honestly, that's probably the reason she talked to me at all. Out of pity for my tired, civilian self. I rolled my eyes and started steaming, but I couldn't stop thinking about how exhausted I looked—and how everyone around me knew it. *Ugh.*

That incident aside, the shoot turned out to be a huge success. And not to toot my own horn or anything, but I absolutely slayed the styling. My new supermodel friend looked outrageous in a belted espresso-brown suit that was so oversized it hung around her like a royal gown, transforming this traditionally masculine silhouette into a powerful eleganza moment.

I should have been over the moon, but I was so tired I barely got to enjoy it. And to make things worse, all I could think about was what my boss had said. With every camera flash, I caught a little bit of my reflection in the metal clothes rack and thought, *Tired, tired, tired.* Plus, because I was just a junior, I was being pulled in a million different directions the whole time. My boss pressed me for updates on various deadlines I had coming up. Then a senior stylist demanded I go all the way across town to pick up a shipment of scarves for a shoot scheduled in the next week. On the way there, if I wasn't answering urgent calls about coffee orders, I was answering frantic calls about misplaced belts on set. By the time I got back to the shoot, I was somehow even more exhausted—and everything was already over.

As the crew packed up, the model was getting out of her last outfit of the day—another one of my fabulous innovations: drop-crotch pants worn as a full-body jumpsuit. Very bizarre high-fashion couture. I turned around to leave—after all, I had a few more work things to get done before I could finally rest for the day—but the supermodel bb stopped me.

"Boobie, you just *have* to join me for drinks. I've got a table at Carbone with our names on it."

Ugh, how could I say no? After the day I'd had, I could really use a drink. Drinks led to dinner, which led to cocktails with more fabulous fashion people, which led to me stumbling home at five in the morning, just three hours before I was meant to leave for another day of making it in *fashion.* Not to mention I still had a few more work things to get done from the day before.

I took a cold shower, made a pot of strong coffee, finished my tasks, and headed back in for the day. Did you hear me mention sleep? No? That's because there was none. But this was the life I signed up for, right? Everyone knows that to make it in fashion, you have to go nonstop, right? The fast track to success was working hard, playing hard, and doing not much else in between, right? Wrong, bb. And I was about to learn just how wrong I was.

Tuesday morning, a few weeks later, I was staring down the barrel of another packed day. I had back-to-back meetings, a big presentation, and a deadline on a double-page feature. Not to mention a launch party that evening. It was a lot, even for me. But before all that, I decided to try to squeeze in a morning class at my favorite yoga studio. Fueled by nothing but iced coffee and stress, I walked into the dark class wrapped up in a pink matching set, lay down on my mat, and waited for calm to find me.

The class should have been the perfect self-care moment. The stunning scented candles were lit. The soft, ethereal music was playing. I was taking deep, peaceful breaths. But no matter how much I tried to be present, I just couldn't be there. My brain moved from thought to thought, faster than Pete Davidson moves on to another it-girl. *Am I missing an email? Does someone need to get hold of me? Ugh, I'm sure my boss must be texting something urgent. Does she want me to come in early? Should I be there right now?* I was so distracted by my anxious thoughts that I didn't even notice the class was halfway through the warm-up. The room was filled with bbs living their best lives in sun salutation. And then there was me lying on my mat, almost in tears, feeling like the world was slipping away.

I got up, left the class, and staggered down the hall toward the changeroom. I could barely stand up straight as I made my way to my locker, ears ringing. After fumbling with my locker code, I slammed open the door and reached for my phone. It lit up. No new notifications. No messages from my boss. No urgent emails. It was official: I had left the class for literally no reason. I felt sick. I sat down, staring blankly for a few seconds, until I heard a familiar voice.

"Boobie? Is that you?"

I'd seen her around the halls of *Vogue.* We'd been in a few meetings together, but we'd never *actually* spoken, except for that one time I called her scarf gorgina. She was every-thing I wanted to be and more. Smart, fabulous, respected. She never seemed to doubt herself, and she owned her ideas without worrying about what anyone else thought. She was a true queen bb. She had gorgeous intergalactic alienne skin, shining so brightly she couldn't possibly be from this planet. She *always* looked absolutely amazing, and today was no exception. A chic oatmeal-colored ballet top, burnt-orange leggings, and a tight, low bun. And there was that gorgina scarf again. What was she doing here? Surely a woman like her had work to do. More importantly, why did she have to be here now, seeing me like this?

Even though I was pretty much *dying* on the inside, I took a deep breath, mustered up as much fabulous confidence as I possibly could, and said, "Omg hi! I didn't realize you practiced here!" Ugh, why had I chosen this moment to say "practice" for the first time ever?

In her calm, confident voice, she replied, "Yeah, I'm a long-time member!"

Of course she was.

"I'm here almost every morning, but I haven't seen you in class before!"

Ugh, busted. "Honestly," I answered, "work has just been so stressful these days. Haven't made it here in a while."

She turned her head and just kinda looked at me. I knew she wasn't trying to be mean or anything, but the look on her face made me feel a little sad.

Nervously, I added, "I actually just had to leave class early. I have so much work to do today, I couldn't bear to waste another minute in that class." And with that, I opened the flood gates. I told her all about my late nights, my early mornings, and my full days. I told her about all the projects I was taking on and all the time I spent on them. I told her about how I barely had time to grab healthy food, let alone eat it. And I said it all with an air of pride, like I expected her to pat me on the head for how hard I was working.

She let me finish rambling, then paused for a moment. She took one deep, steady breath, the kind that only people who are really put together can pull off, and said with a completely straight face, "Boobie, if you don't take care of yourself, who will?"

We said our goodbyes and she walked out, leaving me sitting in the changeroom alone, her words ringing in my floppy ears. She was right. She was soooo right. I'd always assumed a woman like her *must* put work above everything. Like, that had to be the key to her success, right? But seeing her there, calm and in control, taking time to herself before the day began, I realized I'd been going about it all wrong. My work was working me. And I knew that if I didn't reclaim some of my own energy, soon I would have none left. I had to take charge of my own self-care, because no one was going to do it for me. So I left the studio (class was already over), and even though I didn't get a workout, I got so much more: a whole new mantra.

From that moment on, I vowed to never let work steal all my energy again. But easier said than done, right? Making a promise was one thing, but now I had to figure out how to actually put it into practice. Like, how could I possibly go from swamped workaholic to balanced beauty? The same way my self-care decline had begun: *slowly*. I started with small acts of daily self-care. Little things that reminded me I am worth taking care of. Things like making my bed every day, taking a gorgeous sunrise walk every morning, and cooking something for myself at least once a week—even just some avocado toast. Then that turned into light Pilates a few times a week. That turned into drinking way more water. And that turned into journaling every day. And before I knew it, my little self was being truly cared for, in big and small ways every day.

I even told my boss I was feeling burned-out, and to my surprise, she fully understood. She even took a few projects off my plate and appreciated my setting boundaries. With every good choice I made, I could feel myself slowly become *me* again. And the more energy I reclaimed, the more empowered I felt. To top it all off, slowing down made me even better at the work that had drowned me in the first place. Now I wasn't just treading water but rather synchronized swimming—bringing creativity, energy, and spark into everything I did because I actually had the energy to do so. Sure, I had to skip out on a few launch parties, but I launched myself into a deeper sense of peace.

So to any bb out there giving work or school their all, hear me out. We absolutely *love* a passionate bb, and hard work is *definitely* necessary. But what is the cost of success? Is making a deadline worth losing yourself? Is pushing yourself to get a little further today worth giving up your best self tomorrow? Look, bb. The truth is, work is truly just work. Of course it's important and can be fulfilling and impactful. But most of us are not out here curing cancer. When you strip away the made-up deadlines, the tasks, the recognition, the coworkers, the drama, and the stress, what are you left with? You, bb. And there's nothing more important than that.

Even if you are one of the bbs actually out there curing cancer (Wow! You are quite the little smarty), you can't do your magical work with a half-empty cup. While hard work at the expense of everything else may seem like the best way to get it all done now, it's just not sustainable. Soon you'll find yourself tired and drained, with much less creativity and passion than you used to have. The candle that burns twice as bright burns half as long.

So where to start? Wherever feels right to you. Self-care doesn't have to look like a perfect Instagram feed of sheet masks and baths. Or maybe it does in your world, bb. It could be as simple as reading a few pages of a book. Or as grand as taking a hike at sunset. It could be filling up your water bottle at least four times a day or painting your nails while you listen to your favorite playlist. Maybe it's trying a new Pilates class. Maybe it's dancing in your underwear. Perhaps it's eating a big, green leafy salad or a big plate of french fries. Maybe it's waking up earlier, and maybe it's waking up later. As long as you start with one thing every single day that reminds you that you are worth taking care of, you can't go wrong. One small step for self-care, one giant leap toward becoming yourself again. Work will always be there, bb. So take care of yourself. Because if you don't, who will?

If you don't take care of yourself, who will?

Hydration is the best accessory

Fewer sad days, more spa days

Rest is not a luxury

Protect your energy

Spend (at least) one hour a week in a towel

Choose yourself today

And tomorrow

And the day after

Light

all

the

candles

Calm space, calm energy

Keep your peace

REPEAT AFTER ME:

I am smart

I am sparkly

I am gorgina

The secret to elegance? Moisturizer

Do as much (or as little) as you want

Breathe in

Breathe out

Find your ritual and never let it go

Omg, bb, you are glowing

CHAPTER 3

Make Your Dreams
Come True

Picture this, bb:

It's 5:00 p.m. on a Tuesday night. I'm on the top floor of one of New York's tallest office buildings. I'm focused. Head down, typing away at a presentation on fall/winter trends that happens to be due tomorrow. It's my hot take on cold weather layering, centered around balaclavas. A few weeks back I went skiing and had this moment of inspiration when I saw those fabulously warm yet dramatic knits all over the hill. Tonight I want to channel that warmth and comfort to the tundra that is the city, but with a fashionista twist, of course. It was all very hot bb winter.

I am still working hard on my idea, even though I expect a higher-up somewhere will get cold feet and go back to the usual (read: boring) cardigan roundup. Cable-knit, oversized, grandpa, cropped. Just like they did last year. Ugh. At around 6:45 I send off the presentation and gently shut the laptop, leaving me sitting in the dark with nothing but the lights from the New York City skyline shining on my face. I pack up my structured Louis bag and head down the elevator. As the doors shut, I catch my reflection in the metal. Honestly, I feel less than gorgina in this moment. My tiny body is tired. My fabulous brain is foggy. Then a buzz in my pocket knocks me out of my daze.

"Boobie, thanks for finishing that presentation. The

balaclavas are cool, but we're thinking we should go back to cardigans."

Eye roll.

Bb, this wasn't the first time that something like this happened. And it *definitely* wasn't the last. A shoot that I styled got pulled for being too "risky." An article I wrote on the avant-garde designers of Brooklyn was edited down to a quote because one advertiser called it a conflict of interest. And don't get me started on my ideas for casting. "I just want people to be able to see themselves in the looks," I would say. "I want people to flip through the pages and be inspired, not defeated." But time after time, project after project, my big fashion world dreams got pushed away by the day-to-day realities.

I can't even believe I'm saying this, bb, but I grew tired of it. Tired of letting other people tell me what's in and what's out. Tired of putting allllll my heart into something that isn't ultimately mine. Tired of a world that claims to be about breaking boundaries but is too scared to do anything amazing. I had come in so bright and full of passion. I thought I could really make a difference. But I felt my light had started to dim.

And don't even get me started on the competitiveness. Every single time a new opportunity came up, like a shoot or a story, the whole place turned into a bloodbath. Like if the Olympics and the Hunger Games had a baby, then that baby entered Squid Game. I know a little healthy competition can be beneficial, but to have it every day, all the time, at your day job? It's exhausting, bb.

One day my whole department was called in for a team brainstorm. Apparently, all the cover story ideas so far had been shot down, and the deadline was fast approaching. So it was all-hands-on-deck to solve the problem. Even though this was supposed to be a team effort, it quickly became cut-throat, with each person keeping to themselves to make sure they were the one with the best idea. So I had no choice but to do the same. I found a little quiet spot and jotted down some ideas. Maybe we could feature Ariana Grande but like, without her extensions, to accompany a piece on vulnerability? Or maybe a profile with Zendaya flipped upside down because she's turned the whole industry on its head? Perhaps a Cynthia Nixon power-suit moment? No wait, what about Cynthia Nixon in a *birthday suit* moment?

I was thinking and thinking and writing and thinking some more. Then I did that thing. You know that thing you do when you're trying to figure something out? That slight look up and to the side, just to give your mind a momentary break? Yeah, well, I did that. And only for a second or so. But as I did, I guess my eyes happened to land on one of my coworkers sitting across from me, who was also working on the project. As she noticed me looking around, she shot me a scowl and threw her hand in front of her page to stop me from seeing her ideas.

Like seriously? This wasn't a high school math test. I was *not* trying to copy her ideas *at all*. Besides, I was pretty sure I already had some A-plus ideas of my own.

It made me so sad, bb. I've never been great at math, but I'm pretty sure two is greater than one. Weren't we on the same team? Would working together have been so bad? Wasn't fashion supposed to be about collaborating and coming together? I had always believed it was. But after a few years working in the industry, I learned this was far from true. I shook my head, probably rolled my eyes a little too visibly, and went back to my own ideas.

The brainstorm went on well into the evening. No one could leave until one of us came up with an idea our boss loved. We were all exhausted, but no one wanted to give up first. So there we stayed, in our own horrible corners, trying to outsmart the people who were supposed to be there to support us.

Six hours and dozens of ideas later, my boss decided she loved the Cynthia Nixon idea. After all that, I won. Of course my coworkers came up and congratulated me, but I knew they were fuming inside. It was hard not to take a little pleasure in their pain.

That's what this place did to me. After being pitted up against the others so many times, I struggled not to gloat. But deep down, I knew my win was really a loss; I was losing the passion and love that had gotten me into this industry in the first place. I was also losing hope because, bb, what was I going to do instead? I had put so much time and effort into building a career in fashion. Could I really throw it away? But how could I stay in a space that wasn't fully serving my entire being? My options were too scary to face. I had never felt more stuck in my life.

That weekend I decided to shake things up a little. I needed to find some *inspiration*, something that would remind me why I loved fashion in the first place. So taking cues from my trend report, I put on this gorgina Kelly green balaclava extravaganza and headed to the one place I knew I could find a spark: the Lower East Side. Cue the upbeat groovy music. I stomped through the streets sipping a luscious matcha latte from a trendy new spot. I stopped in boutiques. I admired outfits. I sprayed perfume. I tried on sunglasses. Everywhere I looked, I saw something new. Bright colors, bold patterns, statement accessories. Some designer pieces, some one-of-a-kind thrifts. No rules. No right or wrong. Just fabulousness. And all brought together by iconic people who shined just by truly being themselves.

(Sidenote, bb: It's actually super simple to achieve that bold, pattern-clashing it-girl look we all dream of. The true key to making multiple patterns work is scale. If you're wearing a micro polka-dot top with a micro floral print skirt, it's just going to look messy and unfocused. But if you switch out that floral for a mega cow print? Moooooood. Make sure one pattern is bigger than the other to create a focus area rather than a blotchy mess. It's a simple way to take an outfit from crazy kindergartner to bold royal. Long live the queen, bb.)

Anyway, as I was admiring a gorgina angel bb's *outrageous* red Saks Potts coat with that iconic fuzzy trim, I heard

77

someone say, "Excuse me? I just have to say I am completely *living* for your look." I turned around to find an absolutely *stunning* vision of a bb. She was wearing an oversized hot-pink knit sweater layered over a bright yellow gingham turtleneck dress, with matching yellow platform boots and a cobalt-blue mini bag to break it all up. It was all very farm girl chic meets go-go girl eleganza. On paper, it should *not* have worked. But, bb, she was working it. My jaw hit the floor.

"You're living for *my* look? *I'm* living for *your* look!" We introduced ourselves, and for the next ten minutes we basically became best friends. We talked about our favorite pieces of the moment, shared thrifting secrets, and basked in the glow of this absolutely incredible moment. Turned out, she also worked in fashion. She was a buyer for a major fashion institution, going all over the world deciding what belonged on the racks of the stores and in the closets of people like me. But she, too, had been looking for something more meaningful in her work. She wanted to be more connected to the community of people who actually wear the clothes than the so-called style experts. She was tired of the exclusivity, timidity, and lack of freedom. So she had quit the job that anyone would kill for to start up her very own boutique. Just. Like. That.

I was absolutely blown away. To anyone walking by, we must have looked like two bbs who went way back, now catching up after years apart. But little did they know, time had not brought us together. Colors, textures, expression, and all-around fabulousness had. *This* was fashion. We exchanged

Instas and went our separate ways—released back into the wild streets of the Lower East Side.

For the rest of the day, I was on cloud nine. I can barely even remember where I went next. This could have been due in part to all the strong, luxurious Le Labo scents wafting around that area of the city. But mostly my mind was still in the moment between me and my new friend. I just couldn't stop thinking about it. Not just because I love when someone compliments my outfit—I mean, who doesn't? It was more than that. Something bigger, something more magical had occurred. That rare, unique thing that happens when two bbs who share a mutual love of something come together. A moment when two bbs greet each other with kind, welcoming, and supportive energy, not cold or competitive iciness. It was like nothing I had experienced in the halls of my day job. Here was a bb who felt the same frustration I felt and had decided to do something about it. It was exactly the inspiration I had been looking for.

After a long day, I slinked back home to my apartment and launched straight into my carefully calculated bedtime routine: a gentle cleanser rinsed with warm water, followed by a slightly deeper cleanser to get out all the impurities. Then a chemical exfoliant, retinol, and a calming serum, topped off with a rich night cream. After that I sipped on some warm lemon water and did some light stretching, all to the sounds of tropical nature. Then I hopped into bed and spent the next hour scrolling on Instagram. (Come on, bb, I'm only human.)

I caught up on a few influencer stories, then tapped over to lurk on my new friend. Ugh, she was just so fabulous. Even her nonfabulous pictures were fabulous.

I scrolled down and liked a few. "Ugh, bb, this look is beyond," I commented.

"You literally made my day 🖤🖤🖤," she replied.

And that's when an idea hit me. If two bbs could go from complete strangers to literal BFFs in a snap, all through a mutual love of looking and feeling gorgina, anyone could. If I could make an impact on the streets of the Lower East Side just by following my fabulous instincts, I could do it anywhere. Like, say, on Instagram.

I bounced out of bed the next morning and literally flew into my closet. I pulled out tops and button-ups and layers and scarves and mini glasses. I tried on outfit after outfit, lewk after lewk, but nothing was quite hitting. *Hmm.* Then, I remembered a piece I had yet to wear out: my lilac quilted jumpsuit. I paired it with matching Nike Cortez sneakers to create a true monochromatic lewwwwwwwk. It was perfect, in my humble opinion.

I found the sunniest spot in my apartment, stepped back in front of a white wall, and posed on my light hardwood floors. Then I snapped a few pics. A few head tilts, smizes, and angles later, I had a shot I loved. The perfect mix of cute and approachable. A little sass and a little sweetness. It was just so me.

I posted it with the caption: "Hot take: lilac is a neutral." And with my heart pounding in my chest, I pressed post.

And then I waited. And waited. And waited.

A little *ping* from my phone told me that someone had liked my post. It was my new friend from yesterday.

Another *ping.* She reposted the pic to her stories. "Couldn't agree more," her caption said.

Ping! One of *her* followers had just followed *me.* I followed them right back!

Before I knew it, it was nighttime, and I had spent the entire day connecting with strangers over fabulousness. It was the most fun I'd had with fashion in a long time, but I knew the fun was just getting started.

The next day I posted again. Then the day after that. And the day after that. I posted a yellow-on-yellow look I called a butter outfit. Then an electric magenta blouse with a tiny, red Jacquemus bag. Then a dramatic cowl-neck knit with a contrasting slime-green snakeskin bag. And people were starting to notice. With every post, a few more bbs followed me, joining my community of fashion queens. And I followed them back! I wanted them to feel as gorgina as I did the day I bumped into that bb on the street.

I was addicted to making them feel good with my own comments:

"Wow, bb, I'm living for you in red . . ."

"I wish this came in xxxxs! UGH!!!"

"Um, excuse me?? Who gave you permission to be this gorgina? Kidding, you don't need it."

At first it was just a few bbs, then a few hundred bbs. Then a few *thousand* bbs. The more I stayed true to myself, the more bbs wanted to be a part of my journey. It was so simple, but it felt amazing. I didn't have to ask anyone. I didn't have to wait for approvals. I didn't have to follow any rules. It was just a direct shot from my inspiration to the world. No more gated fashion elite. No more competitive exclusivity. No more cardigans, unless I wanted cardigans. (And you'd better believe it would only be a fabulous oversized cyan moment.) Just me and what I thought was gorgina.

That was it, bb. That was why I got into fashion. Not to go to exclusive parties or be part of an in-crowd but to be true to myself and to help others do the same. To connect with people and form a community around something we all love. I was absolutely hooked.

From that day on, every free moment I had was spent creating looks, chatting with my existing bbs, and seeking out new ones to befriend. After a few months, I had gathered quite the community of bbs. And that's when even more exciting moments started to happen. One day, on a cab ride home from work, my phone was absolutely exploding. I clicked through to find that the Cut had reposted one of my looks! And just like that, I was joined by twenty thousand new bbs. Then one night at a friend's birthday party, I got an email

from Refinery29 saying they wanted to write an article—
about *me*! All of a sudden, some of the most iconic labels and
people *of all time* were interested in working with me. Susan
Alexandra was sending me bags, and Marc Jacobs was asking
for a collab. Cult brands like Paloma Wool and Lisa Says Gah
were knocking on my door. And household names like Prada
and Louis Vuitton were gifting *me*, of all people.

Then the true cherry on top: The queen herself joined
my community of bbs. I'm talking about Ariana Grande, of
course. The absolute gorgina angel bb who, for the record,
only follows 942 people, was following *me*. I truly couldn't
believe it. I manifested everything I'd ever wanted. I was
making it happen. By staying true to myself, I was making
my dreams come true.

So to any bb out there who feels stuck between a big dream
and day-to-day realities, do me a favor. Close your eyes, like
right now. Okay, but maybe open them a little so you can
keep reading. Or how about this: Close one eye. That's better! Now, take a deep breath—and think back to when you
first started out. When you were a fresh bb out in the world,
with wide eyes and big dreams. Think back to that specific
thing you fell in love with in the first place. Maybe it was a
love of fashion. Maybe it was the closeness of community.
Maybe it was that rush you get from coming up with an

MAKE YOUR DREAMS COME TRUE

idea. Remember what you were so passionate about then. Remember what used to keep you up all night and get you out of bed the next morning.

Now write it all down. Every single thing you're craving and everything you're longing for in your career. Then chase that longing at all costs. Send that email. Compliment that person on the street. Connect with someone new. Try something you've never done before. Post that very first picture. Maybe the journey will look a little different from how you originally pictured it. Maybe it will be completely unrecognizable from the dream you had in your head. But I promise you, bb, if you take all those seeds of passion and plant them, you'll have a fabulous field of wildflowers. If you take those nuggets of an idea and put them all together, you'll have a . . . ten-piece nugget combo? You get it, bb. Because if a six-and-a-half-pound Italian Greyhuahua can build a fabulous community of gorgina bbs, you can do whatever you want. So here's to you, bb. Make your dreams come true.

Command the Zoom

May

your

career

blossom

Wear your power outfit
Slay the meeting

Find your angle and run with it

Look in the mirror and repeat after me:

I am

Chief

BB

Officer

If not you, then who?

You could do it in your sleep

You are a mogul, bb

Let's go viral

If you love your work, is it really work?

Be known for something

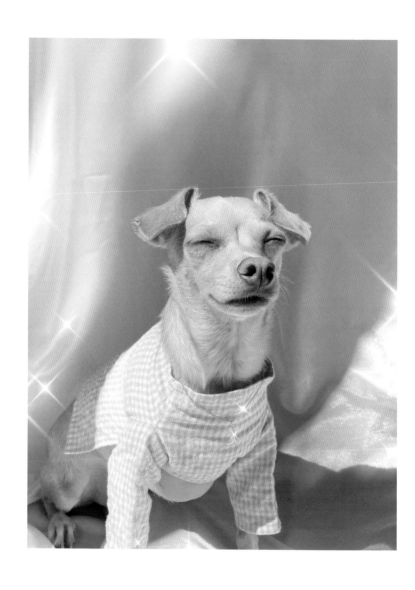

Your energy is your greatest asset

You are a C-sweety

I'd invest in you

Stop dreaming about your life
and start living your dream

CHAPTER 4

Keep Your Bbs Close

Picture this, bb:

It's one of those perfect nearly spring days that brings New York City to life. The sun is sparkling brighter than a Pat McGrath lip kit. People are finally stepping out in their lighter spring coats and swapping boots for sneakers. The birds are chirping for the first time in what feels like years. Is it just me, or do they kind of sound like they're singing "thank u, next" to winter? I'm watching this fabulous world blossom from the window of my small rented office somewhere above Lower Manhattan.

It's not the most luxurious space in the world, but it's all mine. In here, it's just as bright as the day outside. The room is surrounded by white walls, but not the kind of white that feels cold and sterile. More of an eggshell. Warm natural sunlight streams in through the big open window, the gateway for a gentle breeze to flow throughout the room. My giant Monstera plant dances in the wind as the sunlight tickles its leaves. I've purposefully kept the room minimal because I find it helps me think better when there isn't clutter around. A clear room is a clear head, bb. But that doesn't mean the room is stark. I've decorated it with small moments of character that stand out against the white mid-century modern vibe. On the walls, small lilac and chartreuse knickknacks sit atop floating white shelves. A mix of trendy ceramics, flowers, photos, and candles, all to make this little office space feel like me.

Some pieces are more sentimental than others, like the hand-painted ceramic tissue box made for me by one of my very best bbs or the framed photo of me and an old flame. At my feet is a bright-chartreuse low-pile rug that adds a little coziness. And in the corner, the perfect beige accent chair reclined at just the right angle, with a little beige throw to match. It's the perfect place to curl up and take some of those near-end-of-day calls. Getting this just right has been so important to me. That's because this is now where I spend my working days since quitting my job at *Vogue*.

I know, bb. It sounds like a big move. But honestly, no decision in my life had ever felt more right. My Instagram account was growing faster than I could manage. I had so many ideas pouring out of me and only so much energy to make them real. The energy I *did* have was getting pulled in so many different directions. When the two sides of my life started to clash, I knew it was time to move on. No, move forward.

The last straw came in the form of a fabulous opportunity that I almost couldn't take. I opened my DMs one day to find another message from the Cut. My eyes almost popped right out of my little head as I read it. They wanted me to take over their account for a day. The pinnacle of culture and fashion that I had worshiped for years wanted me, Boobie Billie, just a six-and-a-half-pound Italian Greyhuahua, to share my POV with millions. I couldn't type yes fast enough. We agreed on a date, and I went right into brainstorming mode. I would do a behind-the-scenes look at a day in my life, from working out in the morning to choosing my outfits to watching my favorite MasterClass (negotiation and influence with Chris Voss—duh, bb). I was so beyond excited.

But as the day got closer and closer, the realities started to set in. In my whirlwind of excitement, I had accidentally scheduled the takeover on a workday. And not just any workday. The same day Michelle Obama was coming in for a cover shoot. The day would be slammed with back-to-back fittings, approvals, and setups. Not to mention all the prep work that still had to go into it, leaving me literally no time to get my dream takeover together. Both of these moments were huge opportunities for me. And . . . Michelle Obama. Michelle *friggin* Obama. Ugh, bb. I was stuck between the corporate career I had worked so hard to build and the side career I was in the middle of building.

So I did what I always do when I'm in a moment like this: I talked to my very best bb. He and I go waaaaay back. He's basically my life partner, in a very platonic way. Think: Carrie and Stanford. We met in fashion school, ended up interning at *Vogue* together, then worked our way up the ranks in lockstep. Anytime I need advice, I go to him. He's the only one who truly knows what I've been through because he's been through it too. He's also probably one of the funniest people I know. No, he definitely is. So he always makes things better.

A few weeks before both the shoot and the takeover, we met for coffee. We ordered two Americanos and a blueberry scone to share at our very favorite spot near the office. The moment I told him my predicament, he slammed down his coffee and grabbed my paws.

"Boobie, you've given so much of yourself to this place. It's time to finally do something for you." He always knows what to say. Then, in his typical fashion, he added, "And I swear I'm not just saying that so I can have Michelle Obama all to myself."

So I quit. I know, it sounds crazy. But honestly, bb, it was the natural progression. I had a steady flow of partnerships coming in, and with more time on my hands, I knew I could get even more. All I needed was a push to take the leap. So that's how I ended up in my bright, perfect office, sporting a very firefighting CEO chic lewk with a pair of red knit trousers, a red power turtleneck, and a red trench to match. A very monochromatic rescue hero moment. I was on a call with some fabulous editors at *WWD*, just one of a few interviews I had that day asking me all about my account. "Why did you start it in the first place?" they wanted to know.

I told them I wanted to create a space where fashion can be fun again. They asked how I was handling my seemingly instant rise to Instagram fame. "My bbs are all so loving and positive," I told them. "It's been absolutely perfect."

Then the question I had been waiting for: "Boobie, you've literally blown up in the past few months. We have to know. What's next?"

There it was. I smiled to myself, butterflies flapping their colorful wings in my stomach. Sometime over the course of the past few months, I'd realized that I didn't just want to show off stunning looks to *inspire* my bbs; I wanted to actually *make* those looks too. I had been quietly creating a gorgina line of accessories based off my signature looks: mini bags called "Boobie Bags" and silk scarves called "Boobushkas." The sets would be available in four colorways: Pickled Zebra (a bright-chartreuse zebra print), Boobie's Tooth (a lilac houndstooth), Cow Cow (a black-and-white cow print actually made out of the shape of cows), and Butter (a pale-yellow background with the word *Butter* in red). And what would I call this fabulous brand, you ask? Drumroll, please . . . *Boobie*. Has a nice ring to it, *non*? Iconic and simple, like Gucci or Valentino.

I could just see it so clearly. Boobie on a big billboard watching over Soho. Boobie opening New York Fashion Week. Boobie perched above a fabulous boutique on Melrose. *Eek!*

Up until that moment, the whole thing had been a total secret to the outside world. But I decided I was ready to make it known. I figured it would give me a little extra spark to make it happen.

I took a deep breath and said, "Bbs, I'm launching my own brand." And with that, it was official.

They gasped, and I went on to explain. "It's dropping in September, so keep your eyes peeled." My deadline was set. I finished the interview and sat back in my chair. The easy part was over. Now it was time for the hard part: actually making this brand real. There were bags to make, photoshoots to plan, coffees to live off of. I had so much work ahead of me and only one way to get it all done. It was off to the races, bb.

Over the next few months, creating Boobie World became all I cared about. I had a vision, and I would follow it no matter what. I was like a dog with a bone, so to speak. I knew the launch needed to be *iconic*. I wanted the experience to be as seamless as Glossier, the bags to be as iconic as Jaquemus, and the campaign to be as viral as Kylie's lip kits. As you can see, I had big ambitions. So I put my head down and got to work.

I spent every day working nonstop in my office. Then at around six, I headed over to this quaint Italian restaurant up the street from my apartment and spent the night doing even more work over a plate of spaghetti al limone and a glass of pinot grigio. Days went by where no one would hear from me. My phone had so many missed calls and unanswered texts it became overwhelming to even look at. But I was focused. I had to figure out every single thing that went into making a brand. My never-ending to-do list had become my best friend. And it left me with very little energy for anything else in my life. Like, say, my actual friends.

Now, bb, let me first say that I have the *most* supportive friends on planet earth. They were beyond there for me. They knew I was in over my head, and they jumped right in the deep end with me. One friend helped me find studio space. Another friend designed logos. And a few even modeled for my shoots. *They* were amazing. It was *me* who was a little less than fabulous.

My best bbs and I had a standing Sunday brunch at our favorite local spot, the Butcher's Daughter. It was our moment to catch up and share everything, á la *Sex and the City* (*not* the reboot). It was *sacred*. I had never missed a brunch to date. But as things picked up with the brand, that changed. I opened my eyes Sunday morning, immediately thinking of all the things I needed to do, and texted the group chat with my tail between my legs. "Ugh, please don't kill me, bbs, but I can't make it today. Next week, I PROMISE."

Next Sunday rolled around, and same story. I just couldn't imagine sitting there, having a fabulous time, knowing all the work I had ahead of me. And of course, my gorgina angel bbs were very understanding. But I knew they weren't loving it. And it wasn't just the brunches. I started opting out of everything. Casual movie nights, charcuterie parties, and gorgeous dinners all came and went without me there. A few months of this, and I was on thin ice for sure.

After a while of my not showing up to different gatherings, the invitations grew sparse, and of course I understood. I didn't like having to bail as much as they didn't like me bailing. But it was hard. I would lie in bed after another long nonstop workday and tap through my bbs' Insta stories to see little get-togethers, group pics, and cute coffee dates all happening without me. And I would cry. Of course I was happy they were having a fabulous time. I wasn't mad. I was exhausted.

And I was lonely. I missed them so much. I missed the moments we used to have before my brain became completely consumed with building my empire. I missed laughing and staying up late without a care in the world. I just wanted to text them so badly and tell them I loved them. I wanted them back in my life and on this journey with me. I would go visit my fabricator to see samples and wish I could send pics of all the gorgina bags I was making. But it felt wrong to cold-call them, even if it was about something exciting.

This won't last forever, I told myself. *Soon I'll be done with all this work and back to galivanting with my gorls.*

Deep down, I wasn't so sure. I wiped my tears and responded to a story where two of my friends were sharing a plate of fries at a cute wine bar. "You both look absolutely gorgina," I wrote.

"Wish you were here ," she replied. *Me too, bb. Me too.*

✧

There was one big event I *was* invited to: the birthday weekend of my best bb, the same friend who told me to quit *Vogue* and chase my dreams. The plan had been in place for months. We were going to celebrate with all our other very best bbs upstate at this stunning apple orchard owned by one of our friend's parents. It was a magical space—part industrial chic, part modern haven, part country getaway. We'd pack our most glamorous outfits, sip champagne, and laugh the night away. We'd take fabulous hikes through the woods and breathe in that clear, non–New York City air. I had even booked us a massage package at this little Scandinavian spa near the house. It was going to be perfect. It was *supposed* to be perfect.

But a few days before we were slated to leave, I got a phone call from the photographer I had hired to shoot my big brand campaign. She was *beyond* incredible. Her unique editorial-meets-streetwear style had been on my brand vision board since day one, so when she agreed to work together, I was floored. The second I saw her name pop up on my phone, I knew there was trouble. And sadly, I was right. She had some scheduling issues and needed to move the shoot to that weekend. Yes, my friend's birthday weekend. Ugh, bb, I felt nauseated.

I reallllllly wanted to work with this talented queen—but what about my bb? That sweet, gorgina angel who never let me down? He was there to hold my ears when I got a little too wild at those fashion school parties. He was there to listen to hours of crying and hysteria when my evil ex broke my heart. He shared all my posts, answered all my calls. I was so looking forward to celebrating *him* this time! It wasn't an easy decision, but I did what I thought I had to do, even if I'm not proud of it. I just hoped my bb would understand.

I took him out for a coffee and broke the news. He tried

to be nice about it, but he was obviously disappointed. I promised to make it up to him. He silently nodded. Suddenly I was Andy Sachs, blowing out a single candle on a sad little cupcake after missing Nate's birthday, my phone ringing off the hook with Miranda Priestly on the line. There was no place I'd rather be than with my friend, of course, but my launch had a hold on me.

Finally, the day arrived. Launch day. I shot out of bed and put on my official launch day outfit (a silky green slip skirt, a Boobushka scarf tied as a top, and a lilac blazer, all completed by two pairs of white Prada heeled cowboy boots). I rushed into the office and opened my laptop. Everything was all set to go. The publications had their stories penned. The influencers had their packages to post. All I had to do was go live with the website and post on my own page. At 9:00 a.m., I launched it all and sat back to wait. Instantly the comments poured in:

"Bb, this is iconic!!!"

"Literally the moment we've all been waiting for."

"Omg BOOBIE! You. Did. It!!!"

I watched the website traffic. Every second, more and more people were on my site, looking at my brand. After months and months of hard work, late nights, stress, and pressure, everything was going perfectly. I was super proud of myself. I had done something I'd always dreamed of. I had a vision, and I brought it to life. But even while my wildest dreams came true before my eyes, I couldn't help but feel a little . . . empty. Something was missing. As I sat there in my gorgeous, bright office, watching the fruits of my labor literally ripen and turn into a gorgina little fruit tart, I realized I was alone. There was no one there to share a slice with me.

Launch day came to an end, and I left the office. It had been a long day. Tbh, it had been a long year. All I wanted to do was sleep and maybe cry a little. But I figured I would take myself out for one last spaghetti al limone to celebrate the incredible feat of the launch. The bell on the door jingled as I made my way into the restaurant. I smiled at the hostess, and she led me to my usual table in the back. As I got closer to the booth I had called home every night for the past six months, I stopped in my tracks. There, in that little Italian restaurant, my little Italian Greyhuahua heart skipped a beat. Sitting in the booth were all my closest bbs on earth, smiling at me with their little gorgeous faces. I burst into tears and threw myself into their arms. After everything I'd done, I couldn't even believe they were there.

We spent the evening laughing and popping champagne and eating pasta. There were balloons and speeches, and I knew I was the luckiest bb in the world. Not because I had the perfect launch day, but because I have the perfect friends. Friends who will be there to celebrate with me no matter what. Friends who understood that sometimes life gets in the way. Friends who, even though I had missed birthdays and brunches and dinners, were proud of me. Who would always love me. For the first time all day, I felt like my launch had truly been a success.

From launch day on, I made sure to make time for all the bbs in my life. I started showing up for my Sunday brunches again, and it made me that much more productive once Monday came around. I rescheduled my friend's birthday weekend, and we had the most fabulous time. I even started hosting Wednesday charcuterie nights to give us all a little moment to come together midweek. No more missed calls and missed texts. No more watching stories of events that I had to miss.

Did I get any less busy at work? Hardly, bb. As it turns out, launching a brand is only half the battle. Once it's out there, you actually have to run it—something I hadn't fully planned for mentally. But keeping my bbs close made it a lot easier to manage. See, bb, while isolating myself from the outside world may have felt like the way to get it all done, I know better now. I know that you can't just put your head down and work for months on end. You need some joy and lightness to break it all up. You need people to talk to about something other than work. You need people to share in the highs and to be there for you through the lows. You need your bbs.

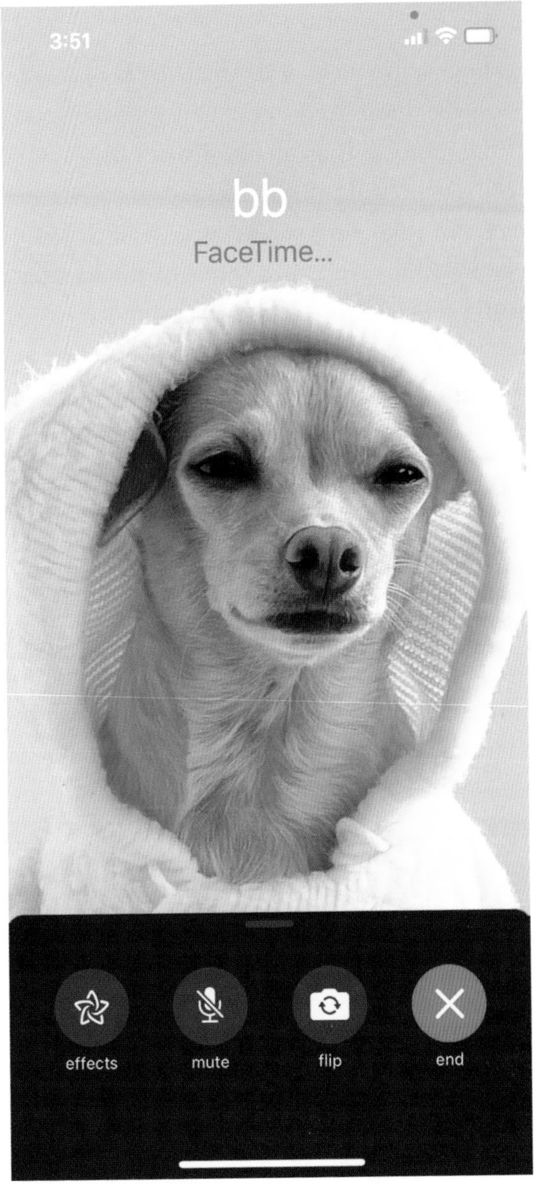
3:51
bb
FaceTime...
effects
mute
flip
end

So to any bb out there with a big goal and big plans to make it real, here's the thing: You've definitely gotta work your little bum off. Do absolutely everything you can to make your dreams come true. Make the brand, pitch the TV show, open the bakery. But don't do it at the expense of the people you love. Starting your own thing is one of the hardest things in the world, but it's even harder when you try to go at it alone. When you surround yourself with people who love you, you can do anything. Instead of scheduling your bbs around work, try to schedule work around your bbs. It could even be something as simple as holding time for a call with your mom or a coffee date with your bbs. It's a small shift in priorities, but it can make a world of difference. Andy Sachs had to learn this the hard way, but I'm here to tell you this so you don't have to hit rock bottom to see the light.

Trust me, bb, the progress you'll make by opting out of a birthday dinner is *not* worth breaking the hearts of the bbs you love. Because while building your bb empire is absolutely amazing, it's nothing without people to celebrate with. No one should be alone on launch day, bb. So make magic. Launch a nail polish brand. Open the world's first swim-up café. But whatever you do, keep your bbs close.

This chapter is designed to help you tell your bbs that you're thinking of them.

Scan this code and send a digital card to someone you love.

You look gorgina today

And tbh, every day

Thinking about you

ma chérie

I'm

falling

for

you

Let's frolic in a field of daisies together

You're on my IRL

close friends list

I love you more

than Prada

Let's

go

do

things,

bb

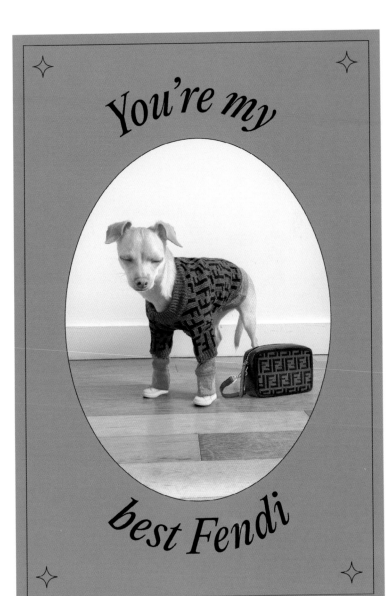

You're my

best Fendi

I love you more

than butter

Be my date to

the Met Gala

CHAPTER 5

Do More Nothing

Picture this, bb:

It's Friday night at the end of a long, busy week. My best bb and I are hanging out at her place. We're in our Friday night uniform: a boxy groutfit matching fleece set for me, and a pair of yellow Girlfriend Collective leggings paired with an oversized black hoodie for her. My ears are in a scrunchie. Her hair is in a french braid. Makeup off, glasses on. We've assumed our weekend identities. And now, it's time to *relax*.

We order some takeout from our favorite Thai spot, pour ourselves little glasses of rosé, and cuddle up on her big beige couch under a faux-fur blanket that literally feels like you're sleeping in a fuzzy galaxy. We turn on the TV and start the process of trying to figure out what to watch. Should we go classic with a *Sex and the City* marathon? Perhaps something current, like the new season of *Succession*? Maybe we're in the mood to cry with *Grey's Anatomy*? Or should it be a girls' night movie like *Bridesmaids*? After much heated debate (I'm always up for some Meredith drama, but she had just rewatched the whole thing), we happily settle on *Mean Girls*, an iconic classic that neither of us has seen in a while. We dole out our shares of pad Thai and spring rolls, dim the lights, and settle in for a perfect evening.

The opening scene starts, and we both squeal. There's nothing more fun than watching a movie you've seen before, if you ask me. We cringe as Cady Heron bumps right into Ms. Norbury in her very first class.

Ping.

We laugh as Cady makes her way through the cafeteria, trying to find a place to sit.

Ping ping.

By the time Regina George is being carried into gym class in the arms of a few hot boys, I have already taken my phone out to check my notifications and see what all those pings are about. Clearly, someone is trying to get a hold of me, so I figure I will take just a quick look before getting back to the movie.

I see a few customer service emails about orders. As I answer them, a few more DMs come in, so I answer those too. I tap out to my feed and see just the most *gorgina* outfit, so I comment on it. Then I comment on a few more posts. Then a few more. Then I answer a few more emails. And by the time I look up again, Regina George is playing field hockey, the credits are rolling, and my best bb is glaring at me.

"Boobie, are you serious? Next time I'll just watch alone."

This kind of behavior was super typical for me. For as long as I can remember, it's been hard to just, like, *turn off*. To do nothing. To relax. For the number of times I've pretended to watch a movie while thinking about work, I could probably win an Oscar. Just add the acceptance speech to my never-ending list of to-dos.

It wasn't always just about work. If I had a free moment, I wanted to fill it with something productive. Like an event.

Or a hard-core workout class. Or a ceramics class. Or a date. A birthday party. A dinner. A book club. And if I didn't, I felt guilty. Even in moments when I was supposed to be "off," I'd find a way to turn "on."

Take my weekly yoga class, for example. Here was this moment literally intended to be the definition of peace and relaxation. Soft lighting, soothing music, mindful movement. Every bb in the class seemed to move through their flow series with calm energy. But for some reason, I couldn't stop myself from trying to out-vinyasa my mat neighbors. I would be in downward dog, trying to get a leg up on the bb next to me. In child's pose, being childishly competitive. When it came time for the teacher to walk around and adjust our poses, I would push myself to throw down the best Warrior II they had ever seen. And when my pose didn't get adjusted but my neighbor's did, I'd silently gloat. Let me just say that trying to be the best at yoga literally misses the point of yoga. But I didn't care. My practice had to be perfect.

I decided I needed to try something new. Something that was purely a hobby, where I could show up, be present for an hour, have a great time, and then return to reality. So I signed up for a ceramics class. A fun, harmless, peaceful ceramics class. Or so I thought. I picked out my very best "I do pottery" outfit (baggy khakis, a tight turtleneck, and Nike Air

Max sneakers), showed up to class, and picked the bench at the front. As the teacher started to explain the foundations of throwing, I had already thrown myself in, trying to lock in my signature vase style they'd write about in design books for years to come. By the end of the first class, I had planned out my entire ceramics empire. *I'll call it BBs Pots. No . . . Gorgina Ceramic Fantasy. No, that's not it either. I know: Vessels by Boobie.* I'd start posting every day with a mix of my own creations and found vessel inspo. Then I'd start taking orders. Just a few at first, but by next quarter, we'd expand to a whole table setting. By the end of the calendar year, we'd have a collection in West Elm.

Wait, wait, wait—wasn't this supposed to be for fun? See, bb, what did I tell you? I simply could not do something just for the sake of it. Everything became a *thing*. An idea for a business, a chance to network, a way to push myself, a moment to become better. I was doing the most, even when I was supposed to be doing the least.

My attempts at not working were obviously not working. So I decided it was time to do the one thing that would guarantee me some downtime: take a vacation. My best bbs and I organized the entire thing. A whole week in a tropical destination, only doing things that required little to no brainpower—specifically, lying in the sun and sipping piña coladas. I was beyond excited. But I was also a little torn. Don't get me wrong; I loved it in theory. An absolutely fabulous time with some fabulous bbs? A picturesque tropical

oasis? A week of colorful bikinis and matching sarongs? Sign me up. But as the trip got closer, the realities set in. I was running my bb empire! There's no such thing as a vacation when you're the boss, right? What if there was an inventory emergency? What if my team needed me? Was I really going to sip out of a coconut while my team put out fires? Not on my watch, bb.

So I decided to be physically OOO without being mentally OOO. "Seriously, call me if you need anything, bbs," I told my team before I left. I didn't even set an OOO reply on my email.

Big mistake.

The trouble started before we even got there. For most people, the four-hour plane ride down would be the beginning of the vacation. And that should have been the case for me. But instead of using it as a moment to watch some movies, read, and sleep like the rest of my bbs, I figured I might as well make use of the time. I caught up on some admin, drafted some emails, and did as much as I could before it came time to stow my large electronics under the seat in front of me for landing. Why not be productive, right? I know, bb. I, too, can see how silly I was.

Within hours of landing, we were at a beach even more fabulous than I'd imagined. The sky? Cloudless. The sun? Shining. The ocean? Sparkling. It was the kind of day they film and put in an ad for a vacation package. And I was playing the part of the fabulous woman walking across the frame.

I meandered down the glowing stretch of white sand, one paw in front of the other, flipping my ears and smiling warmly as I stared out at a horizon that seemed to go on forever. Luscious palm trees swayed in the background, and dolphins jumped out of the water to give me a little kiss on the cheek. Okay, that part may be slightly exaggerated, but honestly, that was the vibe of the day. I was in my absolute favorite lilac string bikini, giving "beach goddess mermaid queen on her way to model for Fenty."

(Sidenote, bb: You absolutely need a bikini that makes you feel like that. And don't you dare start with that beach body BS. You are the most fabulous bb I've ever seen, and the world needs to know. A little tip if bathing suit shopping stresses you out: Buy a few different suits online from a brand with a great return policy, then try them on at home. Do it when you're in a fab mood, put on some gorgeous music, and model them in the mirror like the fine specimen you are. Trust me. It's soooo much better than those horrible fluorescent changeroom dramas.)

Anyway. I wandered back to my little beach chair, where a refreshing piña colada was waiting for me.

Ping.

A gentle breeze flowed by, bringing the subtle smell of salt and ocean right into my snout.

Ping.

I lay back on my towel and watched as a few of my best bbs frolicked in the ocean, splashing one another and laughing without a care in the world.

Ping ping ping.

I couldn't ignore my phone any longer. I would just check it quickly, then go back to my relaxation. No big deal at all! But of course, the moment my brain switched back into work mode, it was hard to bring it back to lying-on-the-beach mode.

This set the tone for the rest of my "vacation." I would wake up earlier than everyone else to sneak in a few emails. Instead of spending breakfast enjoying scrambled eggs, I spent it scrambling to find good Wi-Fi, catching bits and pieces of Zoom conversations between bites of tropical fruit. I'd jump into the pool, then jump into a few meetings. *No big,* I thought. *So what if I have to check in now and then?* I was still getting some fun vacation time without sacrificing work, right? Honestly, wrong. It wasn't just "now and then." I took calls with my team as my bbs played beach volleyball. I reviewed sales sheets as my bbs looked for shells. Sure, I got a tan, but I did it all while trying to get a ton done. By the time the evenings came around, I was exhausted from trying to sneak fun around work. Or was I sneaking work around fun?

The week flew by, and it was time to leave our tropical paradise. And just like that, I was back home, slumped on the couch. I didn't have the energy to start unpacking, so I sat there scrolling on Insta for a bit. I came across one of my bb's stories from the trip—a photo dump of all the fabulous things we did. I started tapping through, smiling at all the fun we had. My bbs looked so gorgina, their hair shiny and their skin healthy.

But as I kept tapping, my smile started to fade. Where was I? *Tap.* Still no sign of me. *Tap. Tap. Tap.* I didn't even remember meeting those guys! *Tap.* When did they get ceviche? *Tap.* Her story ended, all without a single hint that I had been there at all. Because, honestly, I hadn't been. In my attempts to be there for my team no matter what, I had completely defeated the purpose of being away in the first place. And now, after a week spent trying to be both on and off at the same time, I felt like I could really use a vacation.

The next morning, I woke up late. I had ambitiously booked a bootcamp class, thinking I would kick-start my post-vacation cleanse with a big workout—but I had already missed that by a long shot. I dragged myself to the kitchen, poured myself a cup of coffee, and sat down in front of my computer, lazily clicking through some of the emails I somehow missed. I was soooo not ready to go back to work. People were going to ask about my trip, and I would have to lie and tell them it was great.

My eyes started to well up. *I really wish I had just one more week away,* I thought as the tears rolled down my cheeks. As I wiped them away, I wondered: *What if I didn't go back right away? What if I did take a few more days? After all, I spent my entire vacation working. It's almost like I didn't even really take the week off, right? Maybe I could just take a few more days. And this time, I can really be off.*

The more I thought about it, the more excited I got. And it became clear how badly I needed to do this. So I started putting the pieces in place. I emailed my team telling them my plan. And this time, I made it clear. I was *off.* "Don't call. Don't email. Don't text. Don't DM." I even deleted all work apps from my phone, just to make sure success was guaranteed. I put my notifications on Do Not Disturb, turned off all alarms, and prepared to spend a few days doing something I hadn't done in years: nothing.

For the next three days, that's exactly what I did. I slept in without feeling bad about it. I watched movies without checking my phone once. I baked a loaf of banana bread without starting an Instagram account for my baking. I took long showers, spent the day in my robe, lay in bed, and listened to music. I went to the park, read, watched the clouds, and took deep breaths. And at the end of the three days, I actually felt rested for the first time in years. From that moment on, I vowed to do a lot more nothing.

So to any bb out there truly doing the most at all times, honestly—and I mean this in the nicest way possible—stop. Seriously. Stop optimizing every moment. Stop trying to turn everything into a side business. Just stop. Not every moment has to be used "wisely." I know, it feels like you should be doing something at all times, but you really don't, bb.

Literally, I wish the word *should* didn't even exist. Because if you spend all your time doing something, and all your downtime worrying that you *should* be doing something, you never really get a break. You can't be on all the time.

Think about it this way: stopping is the best way to keep going. Taking a break, resting, turning off. It all helps you be a better bb when you finally come back on. So how do you set yourself up for successful nothingness? With a little preparation. Before you go on vacation, empower your teams and coworkers to move forward without you. Maybe this means a little extra work before you go, but then when it's time to turn off, it's *on*. Turn off your notifications. Delete email and work messaging apps. Out of sight, out of mind, bb. And don't just give yourself space when you're on vacation. Try not filling every second of your weekends with activities. Reserve one weekend morning for spending time alone in peace. Take a few weeks off from dating. And for the love of everything that's gorgina, you don't have to win your yoga class. You can do this, bb. *Nothing* is more important than staying connected to your job. *Nothing* is more important than answering emails. *Nothing* is more important than checking in on your project. Now read that all again. It's time to do more *nothing*.

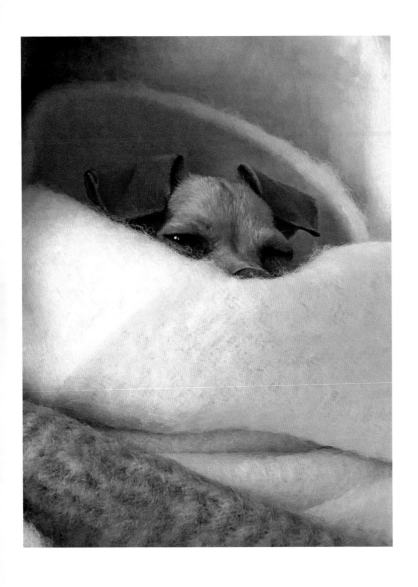

Nothing feels as good as nothing

You don't have to earn relaxation, bb
(even thought you've earned it)

Trust me, the world can wait

Sunbathing is a valid hobby

There's no such thing as *should*

Sleep on it, bb

Perfect your resting rest face

Rest today, shine tomorrow

You can't always be building your empire

What you don't do is just as
important as what you do

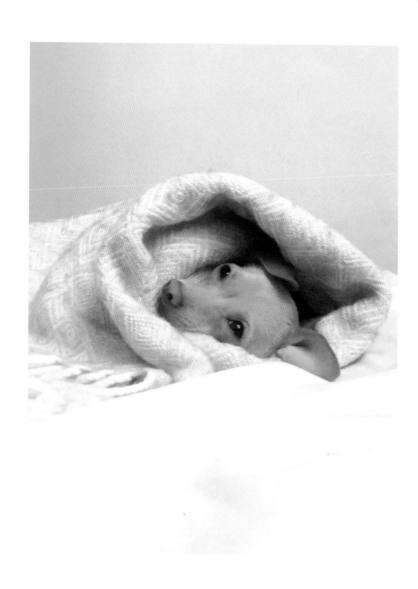

Eye bags are so not Chanel

Take a *real* vacation, bb

Resting is a lifestyle

Never underestimate the power of lounging

Sleep

all

day

On your mark. Get set. Rest.

CHAPTER 6

Pick Me. Choose Me.
Love Me.

Picture this, bb:

It's a beautiful day in Brooklyn. I'm sitting on a gorgeous pink gingham picnic blanket in the middle of Prospect Park with a few of my very best sun bbs. I'm dressed for a casual Saturday—a striped pink sundress with frilly sleeves and a shiny, golden straw hat with a matching straw bag. Very farmers market dream girl. We're sipping cans of tropical-flavored Recess, throwing our heads back, and honestly living our best lives. As I wipe the tears of laughter from my eyes, I notice a man walking toward us. Someone I recognize but can't quite place. Regardless of where I know him from, I instantly know I want to get to know him even better. If you catch my drift.

He's tall with silver hair that blows in the wind and a smile that feels calm and peaceful. He's wearing a light long-sleeve that perfectly hugs his arms—which, by the way, look like they were literally created to hold someone. I find myself wishing that someone was me. As he walks, the grass parts around him, and butterflies guide him toward me. The clouds in the sky coordinate with the sun to create a rainbow of light that hits his face just as it should. All of the birds in the park abandon their usual tune for Etta James's "At Last!"

Then I snap back to reality and realize I'm smiling awkwardly at him. And all at once, it hits me. He's an actor, famous for playing a big ad exec in an iconic TV show. What is *he* doing here? Big, famous actors like him don't hang out here. Shouldn't he be on a rooftop lounge somewhere?

Just as I expect him to walk right past us, he waves. To my surprise, bb, my friend waves back. Have I unknowingly entered some alt universe? One where my friends are friends with famous people? My heart starts pounding as he takes a seat next to me on the lilac gingham blanket and introduces himself.

His name is . . . well, for the sake of the story, let's just call him Mr. S. He knew my friend from a movie they both worked on. They had been trying to connect for a few weeks, so when she found out he was in the neighborhood, she invited him to stop by. My friend went around introducing us, and when she got to me, Mr. S held out his hand. I took it, shaking it slowly and looking into his eyes for what literally felt like a year. Even though my friends were there, too, for a moment it truly felt like we were the only two people in the park. Maybe in all of Brooklyn.

We let go of each other's hands and re-entered the conversation, but, bb—I could still feel the weight of his hand in mine.

We spent the rest of the afternoon sharing stories and getting to know each other. We bonded over our mutual obsession with watching airplanes go by. Like, where were they going? And who were they carrying? We both thought it was just fabulous that right above us, any person could be starting a life-changing trip to, say, Sicily. Or that Channing

174

Tatum could be flying across the country to visit his favorite waterfall. Truly anything is possible, bb. He seemed genuinely interested in my business and didn't even try to mansplain it to me. I know, sounds like a low bar, but *you* try dating in New York. I mentioned that I just absolutely looooovee Frank Ocean, and he just happened to have an extra ticket to his show in Brooklyn the next week. He suggested we go together. I protested—I couldn't possibly!—but when he insisted, of course I said yes.

Day turned to late afternoon, which turned into early evening. We looked around and realized we were one of the last friend groups in the park, so we decided to make our move. We all stopped for handrolls at our favorite sushi spot down the street, all of which he paid for. Then we grabbed a scoop of ice cream at this absolutely divine place right next door. His treat again. All of a sudden, it was almost 10:00 p.m.

One by one my friends said their goodbyes and headed off on their respective subway journeys, leaving me alone with Mr. S. He offered to drive me home in his jet-black BMW, and I took him up on it, thinking to myself, *Who owns a car, let alone* that *car, in New York?* He walked me to my doorstep, and we hugged goodbye. And in the words of Drake, *Nothing Was the Same.*

The next morning I got a text from my friend. "Omg Boobie, what happened between you two after we left?!?!"

Nothing, I assured her, but I was curious why she was asking.

"He just texted me and said he's pretty sure he met the love of his life."

I read her text over and over, my brain really trying to grasp what she had said. We all have those moments where we meet someone who just instantly feels right—like they were made for you, and you two were just meant to cross paths all along. Those electric meetings where your body feels like it's both on fire and on ice at the same time—magnetic energy pulling you into each other's orbit. It's easy to brush those moments off as a one-sided, all-in-your-head kind of thing. But here was proof that if you feel it, they probably feel it too. I felt it, and so did he.

Just as I was processing all of this, a message from Mr. S popped up on my phone. "I now officially look at my life in two ways. Before I met you, and after." I couldn't stop smiling the rest of the day.

From that moment on, we basically texted nonstop. He'd greet me first thing every morning with a different way to welcome me to the day. And we'd go back and forth until late every night. But the next time we actually saw each other in person was the evening of the Frank Ocean concert. I woke up that morning with a nervous feeling in the pit of my stomach. I knew I wanted to feel (and look) my best that night, so I cleared my schedule and planned to spend the entire day getting ready for the evening.

I started with a little morning exercise to get my blood flowing and work out some of that overnight puffiness. A quick thirty-minute HIIT followed by a mega stretch did the trick, with the added benefit of working through some of my nerves. I took a long, hot shower, complete with a cleansing shampoo and a deep-conditioning mask, all sealed with a minute in ice-cold water. Then, it was time for my long, luxurious skin-care routine. (Sidenote: Bb, whatever you do, *never* do any intense skin care the day of an event or date. Stick to gentle, calming things in case you have a strong reaction.)

I studied my top shelf and picked out the perfect sequence of solutions. I began with a mild cleanser, followed by a gentle brightening mask, then a calming moisturizing one. I dabbed on a hydrating serum, then used my jade roller to lightly massage it in. I finished it all off with a spritz of hydrating water to give myself a fresh canvas for my I-just-woke-up-like-this-seriously-no-makeup makeup. That look consists of a sheer foundation, some light concealer, a coral blush, and a little mascara. It's all very fresh-faced, flushed, and fabulous.

Then the pièce de résistance: my first-date outfit. I was going for a very "Who, me?" girl-next-door kind of vibe. Something low-key enough for a concert but high-key enough to remember on our wedding day. (What? We all do it, bb.) So I went with this purple and jade plaid mini dress complete with ruffled spaghetti straps, layered over a white baby tee and sneakers. I felt cute and confident. I felt like my version of perfect. I felt like me.

Right before it was time to leave, I looked in the mirror

and recited my pre-date meditation: "Boobie, you are smart, you are sparkly, you are gorgina."

We met for a bite before the show at this adorable little French restaurant nestled in the middle of a quiet, brownstone-lined neighborhood. As we saw each other for the first time since the day we met, neither of us could hide our excitement. He was even cuter than I remembered, dressed in a smoky-green long-sleeve that brought out the green in his eyes. He hugged me. Ugh, bb, he smelled amazing.

As he pulled back, he whispered, "You look amazing." I melted into a puddle of teenage-movie-dream-crush energy. Was this real life, bb?

Turned out he had reserved the back room and had asked the chef to prepare an extravagant feast. As expected, it was absolutely delicious. Course after course of classic French fare. Aromatic mussels and crusty bread. Perfectly tender green beans with almonds. Some steak frites. And to finish it off, crème brûlée. It was heavenly. When the bill came, I offered to pay, but he waved me away. We drove to the concert in his BMW, of course. The show was electric, and not just because Frank Ocean is *incredible* live. We danced and laughed and sang, and I made fun of him for having old man dance moves, which just made him dance even more. At one point, as Frank sang the chorus of "Thinkin Bout You," I looked up at Mr. S. He was already looking down at me, singing along softly. We didn't kiss or anything, bb, but that was the moment I realized how much I wanted to.

We made plans to meet again ASAP, this time for dinner at his place. I guess at some point I had mentioned wanting to bake cookies, because when I got to his *stunning* apartment (which, of course, he owned), he had all the ingredients set out and the oven preset to 350 degrees. We spent the evening baking, and he told me about all the interesting things he had done with all the interesting people. Dinner parties with Emily Weiss. Weekends away with LeBron James. It was all so intoxicating—and, bb, I was three glasses in.

A few days later he happened to be in my area, so I told him to stop by. I had some work to do, but I figured I could spare an hour to meet for coffee. To my surprise, he pulled up in a Cadillac SUV, two iced Americanos in hand with big "get in, loser, we're going shopping" energy. Instead of shopping, he wanted to take me hiking a few hours away from the city.

I hesitated. "I reallllyyy need to edit a few looks," I told him.

But he insisted. "Work can wait," he said. "What's the big deal?" He beamed at me from the front seat of that fabulous car, and I caved. We drove for a little over an hour, listening to Esther Perel's podcasts the entire time. "You know, she's actually a close friend. I have her over for dinner all the time." I acted surprised even though he had told me this before, but I brushed it off. He must have forgotten.

We got to our destination, a stunning mountain covered in lush green trees, and started our hike. We talked the whole

179

way up, even though we were out of breath. I was admiring the view from the top, blue skies and bright-green trees that make you forget all about the buildings in Manhattan, when he kissed me.

Ever seen one of those movies where two people go from zero to whirlwind romance in the span of a montage? Well, bb, I lived that rom-com fantasy. Cue the swell of the string section. Every day was something new and fabulous with him. One week it was a gallery opening for this iconic postmodern artist friend of his. The next was dinner at an incredible new restaurant that was literally impossible to get into—but of course, he knew the owner. He mentioned that a good friend was going to join us, and I didn't think much of it. All of a sudden, I was having croque-madame with none other than Jon Hamm.

One day, Mr. S randomly showed up at my place with a little burnt-orange shopping bag in hand. Nonchalantly, he placed it on the counter. "Happy five-week anniversary, Boobie." It was the exact Hermès bracelet I had been eyeing. We went back to his place (he much preferred hanging out there, and I didn't protest) for takeout and movies. As he was grabbing our food, I found a printout on his desk. It was a reservation confirmation for the Valentine's Day weekend away he was planning at some gorgeous new hotel . . . in Japan. And, bb, it wasn't even Labor Day.

You might be sitting there thinking, *Boobie, this all sounds like a dream. Why are you telling me this? Are you trying to make me jealous?* I mean, a little, bb. But here's the thing. You can't judge a book by its cover. (Except for this book. If you looked at my cover and thought, *Wow, this is gonna be a gorgina experience,* you were right.) With Mr. S, there was so much more to the story.

As things progressed, I realized that a lot of our time was spent on his terms. His house, his friends, his ideas, his experiences. At first I assumed he wanted to take control and show me just how interested he was. But as the honeymoon phase started to fade, I was left with more red flags than red bottoms. It seemed that every time something was important to me, he wanted no part in it—as if he wasn't interested in my life but just wanted to have me in his.

For example, if I had a work event on the same night as him, guess whose event we went to? His. A shoot booked on a weekend away? Reschedule it. My friends were having a dinner party? He was busy. And he made it all so easy to ignore because he took care of everything.

The worst part is, bb, the more he put my ambition aside, the more I started to as well. I've never been a bb who wanted to wait for a man to take care of me. I wanted to build my life, *then* find a person who fit it perfectly. But when I was with him, it's like I didn't have to consider this. Money became no object. I had access to everything I ever dreamed of—just like that. Everything felt so easy; if I just gave in, I could drift into an easy, carefree existence. It was a very seductive thought, even if it was a scary one in hindsight.

I can't even believe I'm saying this, bb, but I even started to put my business second. I know, I know, don't kill me. But the more he took care of everything, and the more he minimized all my hard work, the more I did too. It became easier and easier to take my foot off the gas and ease into a gentle glide.

The whole situation was clouded in that murky haze that comes with being in love with the wrong person. You never quite know how to trust how you feel. On the one hand, this little voice inside me was whispering, *Boobie, this does not feel right for us . . . btw, you look fabulous today.* But then, another voice was screaming, *He's so cute! You feel so special! This is your shot at love, sans Tila Tequila.* I was being pulled toward two different feelings and was never sure which one to follow.

Until something he did made the decision for me. We had planned to host a small dinner at his house one Tuesday evening. An intimate gathering of a few notable New Yorkers—and I guess I fell into that category for him. But I can't stress this enough. It was going to be a casual thing. *Not* a birthday. *Not* an event. Just a weeknight dinner. Do me a favor and keep that in mind as you read.

I had planned on being home by six, just in time to get cute for the party and help him with dinner. But that day at the office was a busy one. I was collaborating with a beauty brand to launch a new line of gorgina Boobie nail art. The launch was the next day, and there were still so many little details to smooth out. At five thirty, I found myself still at my desk with quite a bit more work ahead of me. I texted him to let him know I would be a little late and was super sorry. I'd be there as soon as I could, but I assumed he could handle it without me for a while.

No answer. I waited a bit and checked in again. Still no answer. A little late turned into a lot late, and next thing I knew, it was 9:00 p.m. When I finally got home, the candles were blown out, the dishes were put away, and everyone had gone home. And of course, he was furious.

I apologized profusely, trying to explain that this launch was one of my biggest moments in a while. Something in my life was truly important, and surely he could understand, right? Like, missing one casual dinner out of hundreds could be forgiven, couldn't it?

But he would not hear it. He stomped around the apartment, shutting me out as I pleaded. He got ready for bed without even saying a word. He slammed the bedroom door behind him, leaving me alone in the living room in the aftermath of his anger.

I couldn't believe it. He had wanted me there, and I could understand a little disappointment. But this? He was treating me as if I had done something unforgivable. It's not as if I had cheated or committed a crime. All of this because of one missed dinner? Because of a work obligation? Not good, bb. Not good.

I realized he expected me to be there, by his side, even if something else was more important to me. He couldn't see far enough past his own life to even *consider* mine. He didn't even think to ask me about my launch! Come to think of it, he *never* asked about my stuff, even after I told him how important it was. *Does he literally just not care about my work? I began to wonder. Does he even care about me at all?*

And that's when I realized something big, bb. He didn't want to be a part of my life. He wanted to have me. He wanted to show me off, bring me around, and use me to take on his emotional baggage. He wasn't looking for a partner. He was looking for a pet.

The very next day, I ended things with Mr. S. Ugh, I know, bb. He was devastated, of course, and honestly so was I. But I was also relieved, which—btw—was a great sign that I made the right decision. He took up so much room in our relationship that there was barely any room for me. Don't get me wrong; I love accessories as much as the next bb, but I *never* want to be one.

The night I ended things, I found myself thinking, *Well, Boobie, there goes your chance at a fabulous lifestyle.* Just as quickly as I thought it, I caught myself. Like, *Omg what was I thinking?* I've always been in charge of my own dreams. I've always been able to go after whatever I want. I have been

crafting my perfect life for some time now, and I will continue to do so—with or without someone by my side. To quote Cher, "Mom, I am a rich man."

So am I still single? Oh, you little gossip bb. Yes, I am. Am I mad about it? Not even a little bit. I thought I needed someone else to make my whirlwind New York fantasy come true. But I realized I was already living it.

So to any bb out there in a relationship, hearing a little voice in the back of your head getting louder and louder, I want to tell you something. That voice is there for a reason. It's called instincts, bb. You owe it to yourself to hear it out. Is the voice telling you that something isn't quite working? That maybe you deserve better? Well, I've got news for you. That voice is probably right.

Now, this doesn't mean you have to end things like I did. My situation was very "boy, bye." But it does mean you have to think about where those feelings are coming from. Is your partner making you feel small? Are you giving up too much for them? Are you leaning into them so much that you're leaning out of yourself? Only you can answer these questions, bb. And if the answers lead you to the big, brave decision of moving on, you'll do what you have to do.

Will it be hard? Of course it will, bb. But I'll always be there to dry your tears and brush your hair. Just let me know your fav Ben & Jerry's flavor. The thing is, you're the most incredible, special, vibrant, and wonderful bb I've ever known. You're worth getting to know and embracing with open arms. And anyone who doesn't make you feel like the gorgina angel bb you are isn't anyone worth keeping around.

I'll let you in on another secret. You've been in a relationship since the day you were born. And if you value that one as much as you'd value the person of your dreams, you'll never feel alone. Being in love is wonderful, but never at the expense of the love you give yourself. So look in the mirror and repeat after me, bb: Pick me. Choose me. Love me.

If someone thinks you're too
much, they're not enough

Make a reservation for one

To me
From me

Buy

yourself

flowers

Every day can be romantic

You're worth it
Whatever *it* is

Pull a Samantha
Take your own nudes

You are your own soul mate

It's okay to be obsessed with yourself

I look good in red
And also in blue

I love myself
How about you?

You've known yourself way longer than they have

RIP to bad energy

Spoiler alert: you've been in a relationship
since the day you were born

Ride off into the sunset with yourself

Pick me

Choose me

Love me

Conclusion

Picture this, bb:

It's 3:00 p.m. on a Friday afternoon. And not just any Friday afternoon, but the one on which I'm supposed to hand in my book. Yes, bb, this book. My essays are written. My photos are taken. And they've both turned out beautifully, if I do say so myself. All that's left to write is my conclusion. This very conclusion that your fabulous eyes are fluttering through as we speak.

But honestly, it has stumped me for a few days now. How could I simply just bring our fabulous journey to an end? After all we've been through together, what are the right words? Like, "Thank you for flying Air Boobie"? "Please visit again soon"? Every time I try out a new ending, a new way to tie this all together with a gorgina little satin bow, I delete it all and start again.

And then it hits me: the reason ending this little journey together feels so wrong is because this isn't the end. This is actually the beginning. Okay, yes, technically this is the end of the book. But it's the beginning of something bigger. Our journey here may be over, but yours has just begun.

From this moment on, nothing stands in your way. You have all the tools you need to unlock all the fabulousness that's always been there, just hiding beneath the surface. Will things always go perfectly? They most definitely will not. Missteps and hiccups will happen along the way. An outfit just won't quite land, and you'll walk around all day wishing you were home. A project will suck you in, and you will have to find your way back to the light. But it's all part of the journey, bb.

If there's one thing you take away from this entire book (other than the fact of my absolutely adoring you), it's that you are more than enough already. Sure, things outside of yourself can help kick-start your confidence, but everything we've talked about boils down to getting out of your own way. Your light is on, bb. Everything you need is within. I can already see it, and honestly, so can everyone who loves you. All you have to do is throw open the curtains and let it light up the night.

I could sit here all day and tell you you're ready. Like, "Congratulations! You did it! You are officially prepared to become a gorgina angel bb!" But the truth is, you don't need my permission. If it's not obvious yet, let me make it so very clear: You are already so fabulous, bb. You always have been. You always will be. The training wheels are off. It's time to go out there and show the world.

I'm not crying. You're crying.

So, bb, picture this too: You're strutting down the street in your most fabulous outfit. Your hair is shining and your smile is lighting up the day. Every person you walk by wonders who you are and how they can meet you. Your career is thriving. Your relationships are nourished. Your energy is balanced. You take care of yourself and everyone else around you. Most of all, you feel beyond incredible. Now stop picturing this, bb, and start living it.

Acknowledgments

Spencer bb: You were my literal right hand during launch. I know things got crazy, but know that I couldn't have done it without you.

Bonita bb: You are a stunning design queen and all-around ride or die. I've loved being in a constant text conversation for the past five years.

Rachel bb: I could only dream of being as effortlessly graceful and stunning as you. You're more amazing than you'll ever know.

Barb bb: Thank you for always being by my side through every crazy idea. Don't even get me started on all the dinners and lunches you've cooked me. You are my rock, bb.

Levi bb: Thank you for giving me the room to grow into the bb I am today, without having to ever grow away from you. I think we can do this. Love you too much.

Christine bb: My mustard, my rock. I love you to the moon and back.

Rudy bb: Thank you for teaching me kindness and empathy and making me the bb that I am today.

Howard bb: Of all the things in all the world I love to do, there's nothing else in all the world that I love like you. Thank you for being so invested in me, like, literally and figuratively.

Randee bb: You are literally the wildest human being I know, and the original gorgeous gorgeous girl. Love you so much.

Claire bb: Thank you for dyeing your hands purple and green with me when no one else would. I still use your suggestion box every day.

My twin bbs: My day ones and most supportive cheerleaders. We will always be triplets.

Hun bbs: Thank you for always supporting me and being the first bbs to own a Boobie Bag. Like, you don't know how much that actually meant to me.

Mitch bb: The sweetest, most understanding bb I know. Thank you for taking my wild ideas and making them real. I wouldn't have wanted to do this with anyone else.

New York bbs: Thank you for making my NYC experience unforgettable and helping me feel right at home even when I was far away.

And of course, to Team Boobie: My creative soul mates. The brains of the operation. It's been a hell of a journey, but I wouldn't change a thing. We can do anything as long as we do it together.

About the Author

BOOBIE BILLIE is not like other girls. She's a color-blocking, pattern-clashing, mini bag–wearing queen. She wants everyone in the entire world to shine like the gorginga angel bbs they are. And, of course, she's a six-and-a-half-pound Italian Greyhuahua. When Boobie launched her Instagram account in December 2019, she was just a girl standing in front of the world, asking it to wear more color. Since then, she's grown a community of bbs who love fashion, self-care, and all-around fabulousness as much as she does. She's been featured in every major publication worth tweeting about, worked with some of the biggest names in fashion, and even launched her very own coveted it-brand, Boobie. Do you want to pet her? Be her? Or borrow her clothes? Honestly, all of the above. That's the magic of Boobie Billie.